CURTAINS
CUSHIONS
COVERS
& BLINDS

CURTAINS CUSHIONS COVERS & BLINDS

Jean Nayar

Illustrations by **Lizzie Sanders**
Photography by **James Merrell**
and **Keith Scott Morton**

Mitchell Beazley

*To my dear mother and father
and to my treasured husband*

Curtains, Cushions, Covers and Blinds
by Jean Nayar

First published in Great Britain in 2008
by Mitchell Beazley, an imprint of
Octopus Publishing Group Ltd,
2-4 Heron Quays, London E14 4JP
An Hachette Livre Company
www.octopusbooks.co.uk

Copyright © Octopus Publishing Group Ltd 2008
Edited and designed by CoolingBrown Ltd
Text copyright © Jean Nayar 2008
Illustrations copyright © Lizzie Sanders 2008

The designs shown in this book are the copyright of
the individual artists, and may not be copied for
commercial purposes

Specially commissioned photography by
Keith Scott Morton

A CIP record for this book is available from the British
Library

ISBN 978 1 84533 417 8

For Mitchell Beazley:
Commissioning Editor: Helen Griffin
Art Editor: Victoria Burley
Project Editor: Ruth Patrick
Production Manager: Peter Hunt

For CoolingBrown Ltd:
Art Director: Arthur Brown
Design: Kathy Gammon, Tish Jones
Editorial: Jo Weeks, Jemima Dunne
Production: Peter Cooling
Index: Hilary Bird

Set in Lubalin Graph / New Baskerville

Colour reproduction by United Graphics, Singapore
Printed and bound in China by Toppan Printing Company

contents

introduction

Few pleasures are as continually fulfilling as living in a home you love. We all want a dwelling that is beautiful and comfortable – one that reflects our tastes, supports our needs, and provides a refuge from the hustle and bustle of the outside world. While creating an ideal home may not be a simple task, it is a rewarding one. And of all the decorative or functional allies we might summon to our aid in shaping spaces that make us happy, few are more versatile and reassuring than soft furnishings. Think of the pop of colour an embroidered cushion adds to a favourite reading chair, the glare-control a sheer curtain gives to a sunny window, or the comfort a handmade coverlet brings to a guest bed.

One of the chief benefits of soft furnishings is that, invariably, they're as practical as they are beautiful. Some can even solve structural problems or completely transform less-than-perfect rooms or furniture. A semi-sheer window blind can mask an unpleasant view, for example, floor-to-ceiling curtains can make a small window appear grander than

it is, and a decorative tablecloth can turn a scarred junk shop table into an elegant focal point. Even the grandest houses need soft touches to make their interior spaces feel inviting. Consider the effect graceful curtains give a room with stunning windows. Not only can they enhance the beauty of the windows, they can also protect the room's furnishings from harmful sunlight, provide its occupants with privacy, and insulate the room from hot or freezing air.

While styles come and go, then come around again with a new twist, the trick to decorating successfully with soft furnishings is to weigh short-term rewards against long-term goals when making choices about when to splurge on a trendy or costly fabric or indulge in an off-beat style. Filled with images of beautiful, classic soft furnishings and brimming with practical information on how to create them, this book is

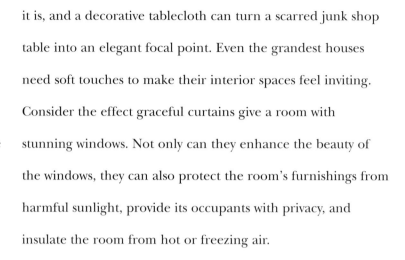

designed to help you understand your needs, guide you through the intricacies of fabrics, and show you how to create soft furnishings that will add beauty and comfort to your home for years to come.

JEAN NAYAR

soft touches

The architectural bones of a room give it structure and establish its character, while the furniture supports its essence and makes it habitable. But it is the soft elements – flowing curtains, plump cushions, decorative tablecloths, classy chair coverings, and fabric detailing – that add sensuality to a space and enrich it with a sense of personal style. Soft furnishings provide the warmth and tactile notes that balance the hard surfaces of a room, making any space, regardless of its function, more inviting and more humane. They inject visual variety, and they perform a multiplicity of functions. Whisper-thin sheer curtains provide privacy and filter harsh sunlight, a silky-smooth quilted coverlet warms a bed and caresses the skin, a rich damask tablecloth lends substance to a hall table, and an embroidered accent cushion adds spice to a monochromatic setting. Cushions, curtains, and fabric covers can inspire a colour scheme or link into one. And – as styles or seasons come and go – they can also function as agents of change that invigorate our rooms and keep them interesting.

establishing
FRAMES OF REFERENCE

above A tent-like canopy was created for this bed by piecing together crinkled antique linen sheets, which were then pleated along one edge and sewn around a top sheet.
right A strip of fine lace adds a pretty finishing touch to the edge of the ruffled flange on a white cotton cushion cover.

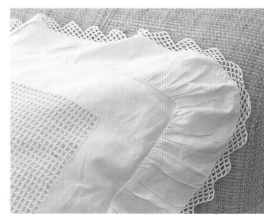

Given the limitless colours, patterns, and textures of the decorative fabrics from which soft furnishings are made – as well as the myriad ways in which they can be pleated, ruched, trimmed, and tucked to create beautiful forms and textures, it is helpful – not to say important – to establish both a stylistic and a functional frame of reference to guide your choices and minimize the chance of mistakes.

Defining Your Style

Before taking on the exciting, but often daunting, task of enriching a room with soft furnishings, you need to take a crucial first step, which is to clarify your personal style. You should also examine the extent to which your dreams and desires mesh with your environs, your lifestyle, and your budget. Do you have a taste for tradition? Or are you a committed modernist? Do you live in an urban apartment with small rooms? Or is yours a large house with oversized rooms? What is the style of your house? What are the tastes of your mate?

Once you've answered these questions, make an honest assessment of how you live in each of your rooms. Do you have a large family with young children? Or do you live alone? Are you relaxed and casual or reserved and formal? Do you like to entertain? At what stage of life are you?

Also factor in the style, condition, and placement of your existing furnishings – as these will strongly influence the decisions you make about the soft furnishings you introduce. Are you starting from scratch? Do you have furnishings that you want to show off or cover up? Have you amassed a collection of fine antiques that you want to refresh or protect? Or do you want to unify or hide hand-me-down furnishings and flea-market finds that have been assembled expediently as you've gone along?

Finally, you'll need to determine what kind of financial investment you are willing and able to make. If you've got your heart set on yards and yards of a costly fabric that your purse just won't permit, consider purchasing a small amount to cover a cushion or two and so preserve a portion of your dream. On the other hand, if your furniture is solid but your rooms need a bit of freshening up, introducing new soft furnishings – especially those you make yourself – can prove cost-effective.

The Overall Picture

Once you've settled on styles and types of materials for your setting, consider the creative role the soft furnishings will play in defining the spirit of the space. Think of your room as a canvas and the fabrics you

above Floral curtains provide colour in this simple room; the French chair has been refreshed with a cream cotton loose cover.
left This extraordinary armchair is made from corrugated cardboard and brightened with a stars-and-stripes cushion.

choose as some of the styling tools at your disposal for creating a beautiful and harmonious picture. But keep in mind a few rules of thumb to ensure that you use these tools as artfully as possible.

The fabrics you choose will be among the key players in the overall composition of the room, which also includes architectural features – doors, windows, columns, and cornices – as well as furniture and other decorative accents – ornaments and pictures. As large-scale pieces, sofas and chairs provide the dominant masses that shape the three dimensions of the room. Covering them in fabrics in solid colours will create the most soothing compositions. Since windows can occupy as much as one-quarter to one-third the surface of a wall, the fabric that frames or covers them will also stand out as a

dominant focal point and should be carefully considered. Unless you really want to make a statement with a bold pattern, again fabrics with solid colours or subtle tone-on-tone patterns are often best for floor-length panels. This will provide a calm background that you can then accent with commanding large-scale patterns on smaller items, such as cushions or tablecloths, which are ideal for adding energy with shots of bolder colour and lively patterns, but will not make the effect too busy.

Determining Your Palette

Since fabrics are among the most versatile ways of introducing colour, pattern, and texture into a room, you can use them to preserve, update, or change an existing scheme. Bear in mind, too, that the colours you choose for one room

will work best when related to those in adjoining rooms. And remember the emotional impact of colour. Studies have shown that red is stimulating and increases the pulse rate, while deep blue, like the indigo sky at twilight, has a sleep-inducing effect. Colours can also affect the spatial qualities of a room. Warm shades, for example, including reds, oranges, and yellows, are known as advancing colours because they appear to come towards you and make a large area seem cosier and more contained. Cool shades, on the other hand, including all variations of blue and cool grey, are receding colours: they appear to move away from you and seem to expand the sense of space.

To narrow the options when determining a palette, the talented New York designers Stephen Sills and James Huniford have devised three approaches to using colour. One is to be monochromatic: to use various shades of a single hue, such as beige or pale

above left A restrained palette has impact in the corner of this room. Gentle colour is provided by the striped linen fabric.
above right White linen loose covers and cushion covers make an elegant statement.
left A good example of less is more. Black detailing contrasts sharply with the white cotton loose covers on this dining chair.

green, to create serene spaces that don't jar the eye. Darker or lighter shades of the dominant hue, such as cream, taupe, or chocolate-brown as variations on beige, provide visual interest. Another approach is to use white or cream as a backdrop and use splashes of strong colour. This works particularly well when you want furniture pieces to stand out like sculpture. An alternative is to indulge in plenty of strong colour, which is a great way to add character in otherwise bland spaces or spaces you might not occupy for long periods of time. When using lots of different colours in one room, Sills and Huniford suggest making them all equal in intensity or value. Limiting the palette in a room to one dominant colour, one secondary colour, and one or two accents usually results in the most harmonious schemes.

If you choose patterned elements, they should also link one or more of the colours in a room. The scale of the pattern is important. The most

balanced rooms include an artful mix of large-, medium-, and small-scale designs, some linear, such as stripes or checks, and others organic, such as damasks, vine patterns, or florals. Consider the textures of your fabrics. They lend interest to the composition, adding to the play of light and shadow that brings vitality to a room.

Light – whether natural daylight provided by the sun, or the man-made light of lamps and other light fixtures – plays a powerful role in the ambience of any room. It will also affect how your fabrics are perceived at various times. Before purchasing a large amount of fabric, bring home as big a swatch as you can get and tack it to the wall or place it over a piece of furniture to see how the colours and textures appear as the sun moves through the sky. Look at it at night, too, under electric light. Velvets with thick piles, for example, absorb light, while sheers diffuse it, and any fabric with a sheen or metallic threads will reflect it.

top left A pair of simple cushions covers get a formal finish with contrasting box-pleated edges.
above The soft edges of the bolster on this contemporary sofa are accentuated by the luxurious tassel fringe around the cushion.
above right Shots of vivid colour have been used to great effect against the cream fabrics in this genteel drawing room.

Living Rooms

A useful way to start to create soft furnishings that truly support your aspirations and needs, is by making a room-by-room examination of some the roles your soft furnishings have traditionally played – and how they can be adapted for contemporary needs.

As the central gathering place for your family, the living room is a comfort zone that should reflect the way you and your family live. As a public space, it is also a place to enjoy the company of friends and, as such, should be dressed to accommodate guests, too. Choose fabrics that are easy on the eye and practical. Think of the inherent spirit of the room, and the spirit you envision for it.

Other similar spaces, such as dens, family rooms, and drawing rooms can be given the same treatment.

If the living space in your home is well-used by family and friends, then more relaxed window treatments – basic curtain panels or tailored blinds – as well as loose covers made from durable, washable fabrics are the best options. But, if your living room is formal with attractive architectural features, and is rarely frequented by children or pets, you may want to indulge in finer fabrics and more opulent window treatment styles, such as fringe-trimmed curtains topped with an elegant valance or swag, as well as cushions made from luxurious silks or velvets with beautiful trims.

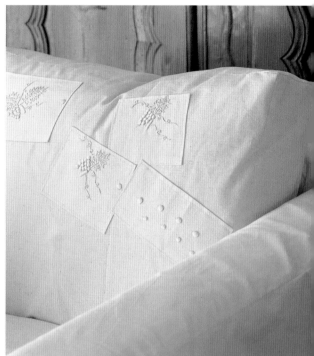

Furniture Covers

Whether your upholstered furniture is faded, outdated, or fraying, or is in mint condition or brand new, it can benefit from a second skin in the form of loose covers. In the same way that expensive clothing reflects the quality of the fabrics with which it is made, fine upholstery textiles, such as wool velvet or silk damask, give a sofa or chair a classy formal air. Cotton canvas or denim, on the other hand, are like a pair of comfortable jeans, making upholstered seating ready for everyday use or giving it a relaxed quality during the summer months when formality takes a back seat.

When furniture covers first appeared, they were simply pieces of plain, inexpensive fabric thrown over upholstered seating and tucked in here and there to protect costly fixed upholstery textiles. Later they began to be tailored to fit individual pieces of furniture – these covers were called loose covers or dust covers. As with changing fashions in clothing, the detailing changed to suit evolving tastes in decor. Simple piecrust

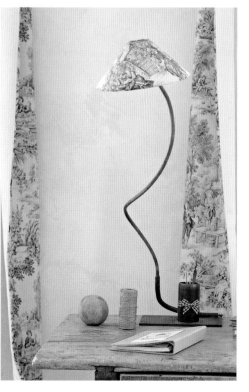

above left Bias-cut piping and a rosette detailing on a bolster.
above right Patches of hand-embroidered linen – a delightful way to add texture.
left and above Lampshades can be linked to soft furnishings in a number of ways: *toile de Jouy* makes a classic cover (left), and swirls of a natural fibre cord provide texture as well as pattern (above).

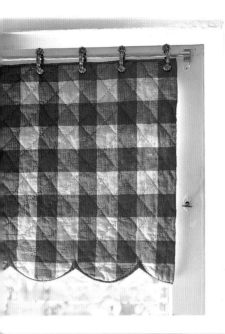

ruffles of the 17th century, for example, gave way to opulent ruching and tufting in later eras.

While covers perform the same role today, subtle details give them contemporary twists. Narrow flanges, contrasting piping, pleated or ruffled skirts, ribbon trims and looped, buttoned, or bow closures enrich them with eye-catching polish. And the fabrics – from quilted matelassé to *toile de Jouy* to printed twill – are often as decorative as they are practical.

Window Decoration

Curtains have long played a key role in creating the atmosphere of a room. They do this through their colour and style but also because they help to control light, add privacy, and provide thermal insulation. During the Middle Ages, curtains served primarily as utilitarian devices to divide large rooms and cover windows for privacy and warmth. By the 16th century, when the technical issues involved in glazing windows had been addressed and windows gradually became larger, decorative draperies in a multiplicity of styles began to appear in France and Italy. This was a period of silks, brocatelles, or heavy velvets, arranged in swags, and adorned with piping and tassels. However, these extravagant treatments

eventually gave way to the simpler, straighter styles of the 18th century, when curtain design was merged elegantly with architecture.

In the early 19th century, enthusiasm for the classical architecture of ancient Italy and Greece ushered in a new era of complex, overlapping curtaining made of heavy fabrics throughout Europe and America. Rods and finials became focal points and decorative fabrics were often layered over sheer muslin and silk "voilages", which first emerged in the 18th century and continue to be used on windows today. During the High Victorian period, revivals of styles of earlier eras were mixed and matched with abandon and window dressings became elaborate in the extreme. Not surprisingly, a reaction to these excesses by architects such as William Morris and Charles Rennie Macintosh, and critics including the American writer Edith Wharton, resulted in a more restrained approach to design in the early part of the 20th century.

In addition to the architectural and design movements of the mid- and late 20th century, social, economic, and political events also had an impact. Curtain styles experienced similar cycles of excess and restraint over the decades that followed. Today the streamlined curtains of

the late 20th century are now being given softer headings, such as goblet, pinch, and cartridge pleats, and touches of trim, including short tassel fringes, flat ribbons, or banding along the leading edges. For simpler window treatments – Roman blinds for example – patterns are also resurfacing, especially bold graphic motifs, such as two-toned over-size damask prints, Jacobean-inspired vine patterns, and fretwork, chain-link, and wide stripe motifs. Today's simpler, softer styles work well both in traditional settings, where they provide understated elegance, and in modern rooms where they add a soft touch. Layered with blinds, they can be dressed up with finer trims to make them suitable for more formal rooms, or edged with simple bands that work in more casual rooms. The quality of the fabric will also dress them up or down.

Accents

Decorative fabric table covers have traditionally provided another way to add a soft touch to living spaces. Throughout the Victorian era, for example, when the use of fabric covers reached a peak, occasional tables were often almost entirely hidden under heavy woven Turkish or Persian carpets. But lighter-weight textiles, such as hand-blocked or machine-printed chintzes, embroidered linen, and paisley shawls and throws, were also used. Today, the trend is for lighter crisper tablecloths, varying from inverted box-pleat covers on hall tables, to printed toppers, and sheer swaths.

Living rooms have also been a customary repository for all manner of decorative cushions that add comfort and personality. A boxed overstuffed cushion enriches a bench, window seat, or cane couch, and floor cushions, pouffes, or hassocks provide additional seating or a place to rest the feet, while accent cushions, covered in antique tapestry or a kilim, add exotic flavour to upholstered armchairs or sofas. They also provide opportunities for sumptuous trims and delicate embroidery enabling you to bring in personal touches that can further brighten a living room with energy and life.

top left Floor-length curtains in a casual cotton check and with matching ties and tiebacks add colour to a country bedroom.
top right Checked curtains and a crewelwork wallcovering set each other off in a spirited play of pattern. A careful balance of small-, medium-, and large-scale designs is key to this artful composition.
above Fine curtains are given weight and colour with tassel and braid detailing.

top left A cushion cover of a brown and white striped fabric peps up a sunroom chair.
top right A restrained mix of patterned and textured fabrics, including chintz and matelassé, updates this room.
above Blue and white checked cotton linens provide a wonderful way to dress a casual picnic table.

Dining Rooms

For soft furnishings in the dining room, the same functional, stylistic, and compositional principles used in the living room apply. And variations of the same soft furnishings are used in these spaces. Loose covers extend the life of upholstered dining chairs, give them a change of garb for a new season, or dress them up for special occasions. Window treatments also do much to complement the spirit of the room, elevate its sense of grandeur, or improve its proportions, as well as controlling light levels or concealing the black holes that windows become at night. And customized decorative chair cushions or tie-on squabs add comfort to hard dining chairs or benches, encouraging honoured guests to linger for hours.

The key to success in the dining room, of course, is to choose fabrics appropriate for the style of the room – be it formal or casual – as well as its function. Crumbs, spills, and other forms of wear and tear come with the territory and so fabrics that can resist stains or that are easily laundered are ideal for these spaces. Also, choose fabrics with warm colours that stimulate the appetite and subtle or minimal patterns to allow the eye to focus on the place settings.

Table Linens

Among the chief soft furnishings in a dining room are those that are unique to dining – those used to dress the table, that is tablecloths, runners, and napkins. Although, linen tablecloths have been used since ancient times, it wasn't until the Middle Ages that they became customary. In some households, they were also an object of veneration, when they were embellished with embroidery and fringes and served as a mark of nobility. Over time, the link between good table linens and "civilized" households strengthened and, through the 15th and 16th centuries, dining tables in grander houses were often covered with decorative fabrics and swagged around the edges. At the same time, simpler tablecloths appeared in taverns and were topped with another layer of cloth, which was used like a napkin.

During the 17th century in wealthier homes, woven Persian or Turkish carpets were frequently used to cover tables and were topped with washable linen over-cloths. These cloths, as well as linen napkins, were often embroidered. The most commonly used material for table linens was damask. Early damasks – woven fabrics with identical motifs on the front and back – were usually made of silk and imported from Persia and later Venice. Eventually, northern European countries, which lacked raw materials, invented linen damask and later, the development of mechanical methods of weaving cotton damask revolutionized the production of table linens.

By the 19th century, checked, striped, tartan, and printed cotton table linens were often used in casual settings, while fitted linen or stamped woollen velvet tablecloths as well as hand- or machine-made lace covers and place mats became popular in formal Victorian dining rooms. During this time, Oriental runners were also common and table linens were often embellished with braided borders, fringing, or crocheted lace edges.

Today, damask table linens are as popular as ever. However, for anyone who entertains frequently, more decorative options can introduce a more festive air to suit the season or the occasion. A floor-length tablecloth, pleated to ensure a snug fit, adds elegance to a contemporary table. A sweeping round under-cloth made of a loose-weave cloth, such as burlap, or a large-scale cotton check layered with a square white topper updates a casual seasonal table, while livelier fabrics, such as a gingham or tattersall check, brighten a country breakfast nook. Finishing casual cloths with ribbon trims, scalloped edges, or hand-embroidered flourishes adds a personal touch.

Similar finishes, such as French knots, embroidered monograms, or box-pleat welting, may be added to simple runners or napkins to tie into or enrich the scheme.

Bedrooms

From the sweeping canopies surrounding the beds of the ladies and lords who lived in 13th century stone castles to the silk-draped silk dressing tables in the Rococo rooms of 18th century French houses, decorative fabrics have long been used in the bedroom to provide privacy, comfort, and style. As it is the ultimate personal space, the bed covers, curtains, and cushions that soften a bedroom should reflect the tastes of those who sleep in the room, as well as satisfy and soothe them at the end of the day.

Since the bed is the focal point and *raison d'etre* of any bedroom, it must be dressed to ensure its occupant or occupants the most restful sleep. Early canopies provided wealthy sleepers, who often shared their sleeping areas with servants or attendants, with a sense of privacy and protection from draughts. During the Middle Ages, bed arrangements in domestic

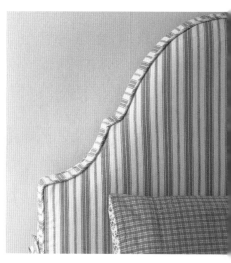

below The bias-cut piping draws attention to the lovely lines of a padded headboard. The blue-checked pillowcase adds a pleasing note of contrast.
bottom A combination of white cotton and gingham-checked fabrics ensures a casual bedroom feels light and airy.

settings were often modelled on those used during military campaigns, and covered with tented canopies suspended from coronas or ornamental wood or metal crowns mounted to the ceiling. Today, with warmth and privacy no longer dominant issues, the rich tapestries that adorned the bedposts of early beds have been replaced with lighter fabrics, which are used now mostly for their ability to cocoon a bed and create a sense of luxury and romance. Coronas are still used, but soft canopies are also often hung from a hoop like a mosquito net, tied to the frame of four posters as streamlined bed hangings, or simply draped over the top as a dreamy over-layer.

For those who prefer a simpler bed, upholstered headboards, bedspreads, or covers, quilted coverlets, custom shams, and dust ruffles all create that sense of individuality and cosiness. Covers for upholstered chairs, ottomans, and bedside tables can enrich a colour scheme or play off the patterns of a decorative pillow, as can window treatments, which may be layered to control light or lined to block it out completely.

Choose soothing colours, limited patterns, and fabric that is soft to the touch to create an environment that is serene and comforting. Any details, such as decorative trims, should be used in places that will not come in contact with the skin.

opposite page A simple canopy of handkerchief linen gracefully adorns a beautiful 18th-century American four-poster bed.
above left This dramatic bed canopy of checked fabric is embellished with appliqué and ribbon and contrasts strongly with the bold floral wallpaper in a guest room.
above A crisp white linen canopy with patterned top adds character to this simple bedroom.

above The windows in this contemporary bathroom get an understated treatment with simple roller blinds in a subtle tone-on-tone print.
right A bold check fabric panel with eyelets across the top is mounted on masonry nails above the door of this stone house, making a wonderful summer screen.
opposite page A variety of checked fabrics have been assembled to create the right atmosphere for an old-fashioned picnic tea.

Bathrooms

No longer viewed as strictly utilitarian spaces, bathrooms have become private spa-like refuges or sanctuaries – some with luxurious dressing areas and enough room for a pair of upholstered chairs and a side table. As their stature and size has grown, the opportunities to soften these spaces with fabric have also multiplied. In these rooms, where traditionally hard surfaces abound – think marble floors, tiled walls, mirrors, and stone countertops – soft touches are especially welcome. But they should be introduced simply, so as not to interfere with the essential functions of the space. Their primary roles are to pamper and provide privacy.

Gathered sink skirts cover gnarly pipes and conceal boxes of toiletries in powder rooms. Decorative shower curtains add colour and zest, and can be chosen to echo the colours or patterns of basket liners or laundry bags. The glass-fronted doors of linen closets or under-counter cabinets can be lined. And airy sheers or simple blinds covering the windows can be drawn from the top down with the gathered fabric panels giving a bather privacy and a view at the same time.

Given the high moisture levels in bathrooms, choose fabrics either to repel water or absorb it. Clean cool colours – like bright whites and watery blues – or pale, warm hues that complement skin tones – like blush pink, cream, and taupe are inspirational in a bathroom.

Outdoors

As eating and living spaces gravitate more and more towards the outdoors, use soft furnishings to ensure that these spaces are almost as comfortable as their interior counterparts. Shaped chair pads, lounge chair cushions, and tablecloths, add comfort and civility to an outdoor setting. While umbrellas, canopies, awnings, and cabanas, define the living space. As in indoor settings, any number of door or window treatments, including floor-length curtains in a covered portico or roll-up blinds in the windows of a porch, control light during the day and provide privacy at night. Draped over a pergola, mosquito netting envelopes an alfresco dinner party with a dreamy ambience while keeping pesky insects at bay, tossed over a table, a vibrant Indian shawl sets the scene for a summer brunch, or slipped over the back of a wicker armchair, a cotton throw provides warmth on a breezy autumn evening.

For soft furnishings intended for outdoor or both indoor and outdoor use, rely on fabrics that can withstand the rigours of exposure to the elements, including dirt, harsh sunlight, and rain. Choose cotton canvases or twills treated with fade-resistant and water-repellent finishes. Or opt for solution-dyed acrylics, whose bright colours are embedded into the fibres and specifically designed to look their best in and stand up to the full-on rays of the sun.

curtains

Like designer clothing, which changes with each new season, curtain styles evolve to adapt to trends in interior design as well as to advances in technology. In the past few years, for example, window treatments have been on a diet after the excesses of the previous decade, and commercial-looking mechanized shades or simple sheers replaced the voluminous curtains, sweeping swags, and layers of trim of the preceding generation. While the taste for more streamlined silhouettes and simpler headings continues to dominate most residential interiors, a middle ground is emerging. Now, curtains with fluid lines, hand-pleated headings, simple borders, and over-size patterns are being used to add softness, texture, and colour, even to minimalist spaces. The projects on pages 40–63 reflect this new direction.

the comfort
OF CURTAINS

In addition to the decorative flavour they bring to a room, curtains also offer functional benefits. For centuries they have been used to wrap walls, separate rooms, enclose beds, and cover windows. Curtains can also ward off cold, damp air, protect furnishings from sun damage, and provide privacy. When backed with specialized linings, they can buffer noise and diffuse light or block it out completely, too. As with any aspect of interior design, choosing the right curtains is a balancing act between your short- and long-term goals and your budget, between prevailing tastes and your own personal style, and between the way you really live and your dreams.

above Lined and interlined wool curtains, with contrasting detailing, provide sound and light insulation in this bedroom.
right Shirred along the top edge, a light cotton curtain is tied to rings with simple tabs and softly filters the natural light pouring through a bedroom window.
far right Made of squares in two pale shades of silk sewn together in a patchwork pattern, a flat panel curtain echoes the adjacent wall panelling.

Initial Decisions

These days, stylistic rules are regularly broken and virtually anything goes. Plush curtains in an over-size vine pattern add energy to a contemporary apartment, crisp linen Roman blinds lighten up a Victorian house, and gathered bed hangings in rich hues give a novel twist to a guest room in a country home (see pages 60–3). In fact, one of the ways designers like to prevent a room from dating is to mix antiques or vintage pieces with contemporary furnishings and soft goods. This layered, eclectic approach to decorating not only creates more interesting spaces but also stops rooms from becoming period pieces, enabling their owners to change them over time without having to start from scratch.

That said, there are still basic considerations to take into account, which can help you select a curtain style that's appropriate to your home, and the ambience you hope to achieve, as well as your lifestyle. First off, while the architecture of a room needn't dictate the style of the curtain, its character will have an impact on the overall design scheme. Do you want your curtains to highlight well-crafted mouldings or call attention to beautiful French doors? Are you trying to correct a flaw, such as enlarging the appearance of a too-small window or covering an unattractive view? Do you have an unusually shaped window, such as an arch, oculus, or bay? Do you want your decor to contrast with the style of the room? The age, architecture, style, and even the location of the room should all be brought to bear in deciding on the curtain style that will best address your wishes and needs.

In addition, choosing a style that's consistent with your aim for the atmosphere of the room as well as your furnishings is also paramount. Few elements have greater power than curtains to affect the spirit of a room. Consider the formality of silk curtains puddled at the floor, tied back with tassels and topped with swags and tails versus the relaxed quality of tabbed gingham curtains trimmed with rick rack, or the dreamy romance of smocked or gathered sheers.

above These unlined flat panel curtains are mounted on wrought-iron hardware. They are designed to allow all the French windows to open inwards.
left Prettily gathered on a flat pole with self returns, fine linen curtains surrounding a round window are held back with fabric tiebacks and topped with a wide ribbon swag.

above Breaking generously at the floor, flat panel curtains in sheer muslin add a dreamy touch in a neutral room.
top right Ribbon-trimmed, tab-topped, unlined cotton café curtains provide charm and light control at a kitchen window.
right Tightly gathered, triple-layered curtains are used like swags to create a relaxed effect in this country bedroom.

Practical Considerations

Factoring in lifestyle and location issues (wear and tear in a family room, ephemeral tastes in a teenager's room, or potential sun and moisture damage in a seaside home), as well as practical concerns (light, temperature, and sound control) are also essential steps in choosing an appropriate style. And, considering that the cost of fabric can range from a few pounds to a small fortune per metre, and that fabrication, hardware, and installation costs can amplify the price tag, it is useful to take into account your long- and short-term goals and your attitude to your surroundings. If you are a serial redecorator or expect to make sweeping changes to your decor within a short period of time, then readymade or semi-custom curtains may be the best choice. However, these tend to fall short of custom curtains in many respects – they're typically unlined, available in limited colours, patterns, and sizes, and their headings

are often skimpy or poorly scaled or detailed. If you choose well, the investment in custom curtains can be amortized in the long-term. When made with classic fabrics, premium linings, and hand fabrication techniques, curtains can last for 25 years or more. If you have basic sewing skills, there are also plenty of contemporary curtain styles that can be easily reproduced by amateurs – and you can save plenty of money, as well as have the pleasure of creating something beautiful.

Scale and Proportion

Whatever style you may be considering, the size and shape of a window – as well as its relationship with the overall room – will affect your options. The area around the window – on both sides and above and below – will also influence your choices.

While there are no hard-and-fast rules dictating the proper scale and proportions of a window treatment, there are accepted guidelines, kind of "golden mean ratios", that can be applied to create proportions that are most pleasing to the eye. Where a window is quite large in relation to the room, its size should be complemented by the curtains and the fabric should be a subtle tone, perhaps with a large-scale or sparse pattern (see pages 40–3). When the window will be topped with a valance or pelmet, designers often follow "the rule of fifths" to determine the vertical proportions of the window dressing. This means that the most appealing depth for the valance equals one-fifth of the height of the whole window treatment from top to bottom. Where there is ample space between the top of the window frame and the cornice, coving, or ceiling, a valance can create the illusion of a taller window, especially if it is mounted with its bottom edge covering the top portion of the frame and just a small part of the window. Even without a valance, a curtain rail or pole that is mounted well above the top of the window frame – just beneath the cornice or midway between the top of the frame and the cornice – will also lend a sense of grandeur and make the window and the entire room feel taller.

When determining the width of a treatment, allow plenty of room on each side of the window for the fabric to be stacked back when the curtains are drawn open. This will ensure that as much of the window as possible is open to view. The rule of fifths can also be applied to the width, with the window accounting for about three-fifths of the proportion and the stacked-back curtain panels accounting for about one-fifth each.

The width of the finished window treatment also helps determine the width of the curtain panels. To determine their finished width, measure the desired width of the total window treatment, including space on either side for the drawn curtains to hang. Depending on the weight of the fabric, the heading treatment you

right Topped with pretty ties, a double set of unlined striped curtains frame a French door. Brass tiebacks decorated with porcelain hold back the outer set of curtains and match the pole. **below** Mounted on slim poles just below the cornice, three pairs of striped curtains add colour to a sunny living room and draw attention to the tall window-seat windows.

plan to use, and the fullness you want, double or triple this measurement. This gives you the finished width of your total window treatment. Divide this measurement by two to get the width for each panel, adding additional inches as necessary for seam allowances, side hems, returns, and overlapping in the centre. The ample width will allow the curtains to look substantial and luxurious and drape nicely when pulled open. Even in modern rooms, where a clean, sleek look is sought, generous panels are most appealing (see pages 44–5). Nothing diminishes the character of a room as efficiently as skimpy curtains.

By the same token, tiebacks or holdbacks looks most pleasing if they are positioned two-fifths from the top of the treatment or two-fifths from the bottom, rather than centred. If the shape of the window makes such placement awkward, aligning tiebacks with architectural elements, such as muntin rails or a windowsill, is an alternative way to guide their positioning.

Fabrics and Linings

In the hands of talented clothing designers, beautiful fabrics are cut, draped, gathered, or pleated into wonderful attire that brings out the very best in the human forms. So it is with curtains. Whether the style is tailored and crisp or romantic and soft, a successful outcome relies upon choosing a fabric that will support the design. Conversely, a lovely fabric might

below Cheery yellow-and-white striped curtains create a bold contrast to the graphic screen in this bright sitting room.
below right and inset A seaside bedroom gets a visual boost with nautically themed window panels, lined with blue fabric and fixed on curved rods with simple clip holdbacks.

left Floor-length checked curtains frame a large window. Sheer white panels below offer a layer of softness and light control.
above Unlined silk curtains lend a modern finish to a period window. Appliqué leading edges and valances with handkerchief hems add finishing touches.
right Merging with the fabric-covered walls in the same *toile de Jouy,* these lined curtains are hung on swinging portière rods.

inspire the design – and quilting, trimming, lining, or shirring can create a variety of dramatically different results.

When choosing a fabric for curtains, it is important to bear in mind its weight, as well as its colour and pattern. Although some heavier fabrics, such as velvet, can be used to make curtains, lighter-weights are generally more suitable, as they are easier to pleat and usually drape more gracefully.

Since curtains often require a substantial amount of fabric, their colour and pattern can dominate a decorative scheme. Decide whether

you want to make a statement with the curtains or whether you want them to serve as a quieter backdrop for other elements in the room. If you choose a patterned fabric, consider the scale of the repeat in relation to the scale of the windows and other patterned elements in the room, even quite strong colours and patterns can blend in pleasingly when chosen carefully (see pages 50–1).

If you opt for a patterned fabric, many designers espouse following a "good neighbour" policy by backing the curtains with a solid white or ivory lining so that windows in different

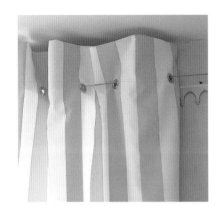

rooms look consistent from the outside. Others favour making curtains with their back sides as interesting as their fronts, or lining them with a solid colour fabric that complements a patterned face fabric (see pages 46–7). If you choose this approach, bear in mind that sunlight passing through the fabrics will produce "bleed-through", where the colour or pattern of the lining fabric shows through to the face fabric, so you'll need to use an interlining. And, unless your curtains are sheers or very casual, always line them with a fabric that is similar in weight and fibre content to the face fabric to enhance drapability and to give them an air of quality and substance.

Headings and Hems

The heading will be a dominant feature. Along with the colour, pattern, and texture of the fabric, it will define the character of your curtains. There are three basic types of headings: pleats, hanger headings, and pockets. Within these, a vast array of styles can be created to complement your decor, be it formal or casual, romantic or minimalist. And any number of borders, buttons, tassels, and trims may be added to offer an additional dimension to any type of heading.

Formal pleated panels are typically stiffened with buckram, and range from crisp pinch pleats, X pleats, knife pleats, and boxed pleats

top Threaded through small grommets, a taut stainless-steel wire suspends a pair of curtains.
above A decorative metal holdback draws this curtain panel to one side, softening the window.
right Attached to peg rails mounted at picture-rail height, tie-top unlined curtains frame a bed and the adjacent window.

Headings and trims

1

1 Gathered pocket
This heading is simple to make and results in a neat finish, without the need to use hooks or pins. Here a tightly gathered rod pocket is layered over a Roman shade; the top ruffle provides a feminine flourish.

SEE **PAGES 52–3 FOR AN EXAMPLE OF A POCKET HEADING**

2 Pinch pleats
Deep triple pinch, or French, pleats are a classic heading for traditional or contemporary rooms. A variety of pleats can be used for headings and give a satisfying customized look.

SEE **PLEATED TIE CURTAINS, PAGES 46–9**

2

3 Goblet pleats
A fringe-trimmed self-valance with goblet pleats provides an elegant heading for traditional window treatments. Triple pleated and hand-tacked at the base, the top of the pleat is left open like a tube and filled with padding to maintain the soft goblet shape.

3

4

4 Gathered pocket with tassel fringe
A self-valance gets a simple soft touch at top with a single gathered rod pocket, which is the very simplest heading to make. Curved along the leading edge, the valance is embellished with a tasseled fringe and complementary decorative ribbon trim.

rings, while popular casual styles include fold-over tabs, scalloped tabs, tie tabs, and grommets. Accordion-pleated headings or shirred ruffled headings can also be topped with bow hangers for a romantic look.

Pocket-style headings, whether they consist of simple single pole pockets or several pockets with ruffles, self valances, flounces, or belt loops, always result in soft or romantic curtains (see, for example, pages 52–3).

At the other end of the curtain panel, the hem plays a vital role. Like a well-made pair of gentleman's trousers, which break at the top of the shoe for a graceful line, floor-length curtains should rest on the floor by 1.25–5cm (½–2in) for an elegant drape, although many people prefer curtains that stop a little short of the floor for ease of cleaning. Curtains that puddle onto the floor are typically 15–25cm (6–10in) longer than the floor-to-ceiling height. Hem short curtains at the windowsill – curtains hemmed between the sill and floor look untidy.

Folding a double hem will enhance the drape of a curtain panel. A standard depth for the heading and hem of floor-length curtains is 10cm (4in), though this may be vary depending on the style of your curtains and whether they are lined. For double-height spaces these dimensions may be increased or even doubled.

above Metal holdbacks in a variety of designs impart an elegant refinement to three very different curtain fabrics.
above right Mounted on the window frame, two-thirds of the way up from the sill, a wooden medallion holdback allows a simple gathered sheer panel to drape gracefully to one side.

to softer, more rounded cartridge pleats, pencil pleats, goblet pleats, butterfly pleats, and fan pleats. For a softer more romantic heading, a variety of heading tapes can be employed to produce shirred or ruched cuffs, or smocked effects. Soft, hand-pleated styles include cupped pleats, rolled cuffs, and wired flounces.

Hanger headings, such as tabs, ties, and rings, atop flat panels are suitable for both traditional and casual settings, depending on the style (see, for example, pages 56–9). They are also simple for beginners to construct, require less fabric, and are easy to remove for cleaning.

Formal hanger headings include gathered tabs, loops with rosettes, and tiered cuffs with

Trims, Tiebacks, and Tassels

Whether your curtains are formal and topped with a structured lambrequin (see page 71), or casual with relaxed tie tabs, they're candidates for decorative finishing touches. For formal traditional curtains, leading edges embellished wide jacquard ribbon trim with Greek key or other streamlined motifs look good. Box-pleat welting, brush fringe, onion tassel fringe, or shaped or scalloped contrast banding trimmed with braid, offer fresh alternatives to the more extravagant fringes and tassels of the past. For polished but more contemporary curtains, wide flat ribbon trimming or crisp contrasting bands along the hem and side edges add subtle

Tiebacks and tassles

1 Relaxed tieback

One of the most simple tiebacks is made using a long piece of fabric, seamed with right sides facing to make a tube and then turned right side out and the open end stitched neatly closed. Suspended from a hook, this can then be wrapped around the curtain and tied in a bow.

2 Formal tieback

Two overlapping unlined curtains in contrasting patterns is a typically Swedish approach to dressing a window. A fabric tieback matching one of the curtains is looped over a metal holdback.

SEE **FLAT PANEL CURTAINS, PAGES 40–3**

3 Padded tieback

Adding padding to a tube of fabric makes an interesting tieback. This one is made of multicoloured velvet and looped over a whimsical metal hook which provides an eye-catching finishing touch to simple yellow taffeta curtains.

4 Tassels

These pretty tassels have been attached to complementary cords to create a classic tieback for elegant floral bed curtains. Although tiebacks are available readymade, it is easy to custom-make your own.

SEE **CORD AND TASSEL TIEBACKS, PAGES 54–5**

The Comfort of Curtains 37

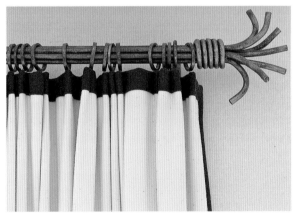

above A stainless steel pole and basic clip rings provide a simple way to suspend a contemporary layered, flat-panel treatment.
top right This white-painted wooden pole with ball finials is ideal for window treatments in relaxed traditional settings, such as a country cottage.
centre A sleek metal pole with classic finials gives a modern touch to casual curtains with a smocked heading and ties knotted to the rings.
bottom right An organic artistic finial lends a note of whimsy to contemporary flat-panelled wool curtains with contrasting borders.

character, while for casual curtains, rick rack, twill tape, grosgrain, small beaded trim, ball fringe, or self valances with tassel trim can add an appropriate note of charm.

Soft tiebacks, whether they are made of the same or contrasting fabric or from ropes, cords, or tassels (see pages 54–5), may provide the only finishing touch to your curtains or they can link with other trimmings to produce a harmonious flourish.

Tracks, Poles, and Finials

An integral part of how any curtain looks and functions is the pole or rail that supports it. If your curtains call for a pole that's visible, choosing a style that complements their spirit is key. Formal drapes topped by a hard cornice or swags can be mounted on a mechanical track with returns that turn back into the wall. But fancy curtains topped with pleats and exposed rings require a decorative pole made of wood or cast iron or another metal and finished to link with other surfaces in the room, whether

they're whitewashed, walnut-stained, or gilded. For contemporary curtains, brushed nickel and stainless steel rails offer a sleeker profile, as do flat or stylized poles that have self-returns in attractive metal finishes such as cast iron or bronze. Painted ceiling-mounted exposed architectural tracks are another option for simpler more streamlined curtain styles.

Whether traditional – such as acorns, spears, or fleurs de lis – or modern geometric shapes or jewel-toned glass spheres, finials and holdbacks

left Narrow poles set inside the window recess complement the slender wooden ceiling beams. The red-and-white theme of the room creates a cosy ambience.
below Mounted on a super-slim rod, sheer curtains wrap a room with classic modern appeal.
bottom Layered over a bamboo blind and tied back with a long tie, a simple gingham curtain helps disguise the restrictions of the space in this bathroom.

should also reflect not only the character of the curtains but that of other furnishings as well. If you want to mount a layered treatment, sheers beneath silk panels for example, choose integrated double and triple rails, which are available in basic track or decorative styles.

When choosing a rail or pole it's also important to consider how long it will need to be, how it will be mounted to the ceiling or wall, and how much weight it can bear. Standard poles are usually made in 2.5–5cm (1–2in) diameters and are supported by brackets that project a fixed distance. If obstructions, such as radiators, preclude the use of wall-mounted brackets for floor-length curtains, you'll need a ceiling-mounted pole or track. Also, depending upon its diameter and what it is made of, any pole can support only so much weight without bending or breaking. If your window is very wide and you'll need more than one centre bracket to support the weight of the curtains, opt instead for a decorative traverse rod with a concealed track mechanism or a ceiling-mounted architectural track, which can support the weight of large curtains and enable them to open and close over a wide expanse without being blocked by a bracket. Finally, using appropriate fixings, including wall anchors, for your wall or ceiling will ensure a successful and functional installation.

Flat Panel Curtains

These simple flat-panelled curtains enhance the drama and scale of double-height windows, framing them with cascades of softness. Making the panels from a solid neutral cotton canvas keeps the attention on the view, but a simple stripe or a tone-on-tone, large scale damask would achieve a similar result while providing subtle shots of interest. These panels are lined with a napped fabric that not only improves the drape but also provides thermal insulation and buffers noise – especially helpful for extra-large windows. The wide tiebacks with just a hint of a contrasting edge add a modern, elegant touch.

MATERIALS

- Main fabric (for measuring tips, see pages 179–81)
- Lining fabric, such as napped sateen
- Buckram, 10cm (4in) wide
- Covered, 2.5cm (1in) curtain weights (optional)
- Contrasting fabric for tiebacks
- Sewing kit (see pages 170–3)
- 3.75cm (1½in) pin hooks
- Cup hooks for the tiebacks
- Curtain rail and fixings. Mount according to manufacturer's instructions

For large windows, simplicity is the key, from the colour of the fabric to the style of the headings. This way the curtains don't steal the show.

1 To determine the cut length of each curtain panel, measure from the bottom of the curtain rail to the floor and add 38cm (15in).

2 For the cut width of each panel, measure the curtain rail and multiply by 2 or 2½, depending on the desired fullness (the curtains shown have a fullness factor of 2). You may need to join one or more fabric widths, or portions of widths, to get this fullness. If so divide your width figure by the width of the fabric and round up or down to the nearest whole number; this gives you the number of fabric widths you'll need. Divide the multiplied width dimension by 2 and add 15cm

(6in) to get the cut width of each panel. Measure, mark, and cut the panels to these dimensions.

3 Join the widths with 1.25cm (½in) seams, matching patterns if necessary (see page 180). Before joining widths, cut off the selvages or clip into the allowance to prevent pulling (do this for the lining too, see step 4). If you trim the selvages, use overcast stitch and an edging foot to finish the seam edges, if desired (see page 178). Press seams open. Note: Consider stitching curtain weights into the seams of the main fabric 15cm (6in) from the bottom to avoid puckering.

4 Repeat for the lining fabric, adding 2.5cm (1in), rather than 38cm (15in), to the length dimension for both heading and hem, and trimming 7.5cm (3in) from each side edge of the joined widths. Press open the seams.

5 Fold under and press the top edges of the main fabric panels by 2.5cm (1in) then 10cm (4in). Open out the folds.

continued over >>

>> **continued**

6 Fold, press, and pin a 10cm (4in) double hem along the bottom edge of each main fabric panel. Trim the seams within the hem area to about 6mm (¼in). Tack the hem, then hand-sew using hemming stitch (see page 174), or machine-stitch using blind hem stitch and a blind hem foot (see page 178). Remove the tacking stitches.

8 Fold under and press 4cm (1½in) double hems along both sides of each panel of main fabric. Open out the folds.

7 Along the bottom of the lining fabric panels, fold under and press a 5cm (2in) double hem towards the wrong (napped) side and machine-topstitch to close the hem.

9 Cut two pieces of buckram 10cm (4in) wide and as long as the width of the joined lining panels.

10 To make up the curtains, centre the lining fabric over the main fabric on a work surface, right sides facing (the napped side of the lining is the wrong side). Align the top raw edge of the lining with the inner fold of the main panel along the top edge. (The main fabric panels will be 7.5cm (3in) wider than the lining panels on each side.) Insert the buckram between the 2.5cm (1in) and 10cm (4in) fold lines of the main fabric, centring it over the lining. Fold the top edge of the main fabric over the lining, then pin and machine-topstitch the top edge of the panels. (The bottom hemmed edge of the main fabric will extend beyond the bottom edge of the lining fabric.)

11 Fold in and pin the side hems to cover the raw edges of the lining on both sides of each panel and tack in place. Tack the bottom hems. Sew all the hems, either by hand using hemming stitch, or by machine using blind hem stitch and a blind hem foot. Remove the tacking.

To make tiebacks:

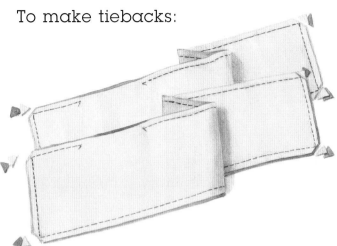

1 Measure, mark, and cut two pieces of main fabric, 25 x 132cm (10 x 52in) and two pieces to the same dimensions from the contrasting fabric. Place a piece of contrasting fabric over a piece of main fabric, with right sides facing and raw edges matching. Machine-sew the two pieces together with 1.25cm (½in) seams, leaving a 17.5cm (7in) opening along one long edge. Clip the corners of the seam allowance, turn the tieback right side out, slipstitch the opening closed, and press. Repeat with the other fabric pieces to create the other tieback.

2 Fold a tieback in half crosswise, the contrasting fabric on the inside. Sew the loose ends together with several hand stitches in the centre. Repeat for the other tieback. Fix the cup hooks into the wall next to the outer edges of the curtains. Slip the tiebacks under the bottom of the curtains, slide them up, and hook the stitched edge over the cup hooks, folding the contrasting edge over along the top so it is just visible.

12 Place the panels face down on a work surface. Starting about 2–2.5cm (¾–1in) in from the leading edge, measure and mark the placement of the pin hooks, so that the top of the hook will be about 2–2.5cm (¾–1in) below the top edge of the panels. Evenly space the hooks about 10–12cm (4–5in) apart, ending about 2–2.5cm (¾–1in) from the other side.

13 Press the panels and attach each pin hook to a carrier on the rail. If applicable, adjust the tension on the cord and attach the rail's tension device to the wall.

Lined Curtains with Fan Pleats

These dreamy, creamy linen curtains, topped with fan pleats, are perfect for draping the windows of a contemporary bedroom. The impression of understated luxury is enhanced by the length of the curtains, which are allowed to "kiss" the floor, and by the plushness created by the napped lightweight lining. Unlike stiffened pinch, or French, pleats, which are made with groups of two or three pleats, these fan pleats are shortish, include four pleats, and have no stiffener at the top edge. They are also stitched by hand for a soft appearance.

MATERIALS

- Main fabric (for measuring tips, see pages 179–81)
- Lining fabric, such as napped sateen
- Basting gun (optional)
- Sewing kit (see page 170–3)
- 3.75cm (1½in) pin hooks
- Curtain pole and fixings. Mount according to manufacturer's instructions

Running across a wide expanse, these curtains are mounted on a decorative pole that can support their weight and allow them to be drawn open and closed without interference from central brackets.

1 Following the manufacturer's instructions and using appropriate fixings, mount the curtain pole on the wall or ceiling.

2 For the cut length of each curtain panel, measure from the bottom of the curtain pole to the floor and add 22.5cm (9in). For the cut width of each panel, measure the width of

the pole and multiply by 2 or 2½, depending on the desired fullness. (These curtains have a fullness factor of 2.) You may need to join one or more fabric widths or portions of widths to get this fullness. If so divide your width figure by the width of the fabric and round up or down to the nearest whole number; this gives you the number of fabric widths you'll need. Divide the multiplied width dimension by 2 and add 15cm (6in) to get the cut width of each panel. Measure, mark, and cut the panels to these dimensions, joining widths with 1.25cm (½in) seams and matching patterns if necessary (see page 180). Before joining widths, cut off the selvages or clip into the allowance to prevent pulling (do this for the lining too, see step 3). If you trim the selvages, use overcast stitch and an edging foot (see page 178) to finish the edges of the seams, if desired. Press seams open.

3 Repeat for the lining fabric, adding 7.5cm (3in), rather than 22.5cm (9in), to the length dimension for heading and hem, and trimming 7.5cm (3in) from each side edge of the joined widths of lining. If you didn't cut off the selvages, clip into the allowance of both the main fabric and lining panels to prevent the fabric from pulling. Press open the seams.

4 Fold, press, and pin a 10cm (4in) double hem along the bottom edge of each main fabric panel. Tack the hem, then sew the hems by hand using hemming stitch (see page 174), or by machine using blind hemstitch and a blind hem foot (see page 178). Remove the tacking stitches.

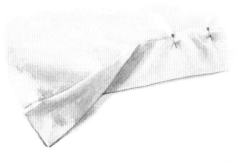

5 Along the bottom of the lining fabric, fold under and press a 5cm (2in) double hem towards the wrong (napped) side of the lining fabric and machine-topstitch to close the hem.

6 Fold under and press 3.25cm (1¼in) double hems along both sides of each panel of main fabric. Unfold the hems.

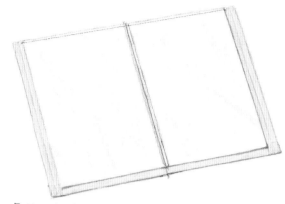

7 To make the curtains, centre the lining fabric over the main fabric on a flat surface, right sides facing (the napped side of the lining is the wrong side) and the top raw edges aligned. (The main fabric panels will be 7.5cm/3in wider than the lining panels on each side.) Pin the raw top edges together. Machine-stitch the top edges together with 1.25cm (½in) seams. (The bottom hemmed edge of the main fabric will extend beyond the bottom edge of the lining, see step 8.)

8 Turn the curtain right side out and press over the top edge of the main fabric along the seam so that 1.25cm (½in) of main fabric appears along the top edge of the lining side and the bottom hem of the lining is about 5cm (2in) above the bottom hem of the main fabric.

11 Fold up the fabric so the first pin meets the second pin and tack this pleat together about 4.5cm (1¾in) from the top edge with a basting gun or a few stitches. Fold up the third pin to meet the fourth, and again tack the pleat about 4.75cm (1¾in) from the top edge. Continue, joining the fifth pin to the sixth and so on, leaving 10cm (4in) gaps between pleats.

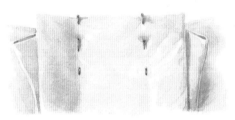

9 Fold in and pin the side hems to cover the raw edges of the lining on both sides of each panel. Tack the side hems to the lining, then stitch the hems by hand using hemming stitch, or by machine using blind hemstitch and a blind hem foot. Remove the tacking stitches.

12 Within each folded pleat, fold in four 2cm (¾in) pleats and join them with the basting gun or a few stitches. Pinch the pleats together with your fingers and hand-sew them together at their front and back edges, letting the top edges of the pleats softly fan open. (Note: the pleats could also be tacked by machine with button-sewing stitch or zigzag stitch with the feed dogs down.) Clip off the plastic tacks if appropriate.

10 To make the pleats, measure 10cm (4in) from the leading edge of one curtain and place a pin at the top edge here. Now measure 15cm (6in) from the first pin and place another pin. Continue measuring 10cm (4in), then 15cm (6in) segments along the top edge, marking off each segment with pins until you get close to the other side.

13 Press the finished pleated panels and insert a curtain hook into the centre back of each pleat between the lining and main fabrics. Attach the hooks to the carriers on the pole. If you're using rings instead of hooks, hand-sew the rings to the back of each pleat and slide them onto the pole.

Lined Curtains with Fan Pleats   **45**

Pleated Tie Curtains

Made from a tightly woven cotton sateen in a creamy colour, these simply pleated curtains frame a bedroom window with understated style. The classic black-and-white *toile de Jouy* lining allows the curtains to be reversed for a more energetic effect. Slender contrasting ties between the pleats secure the rings in place and have been left to dangle, creating a fringed valance. They could just as easily be flipped out of view to the toile side of the curtain panels for a clean, more serene look. The ties can also be tied directly around the rods in loose loops and secured with bows for a subtle feminine flourish.

MATERIALS

- Plain fabric (for measuring tips, see pages 179–81)
- Contrasting fabric
- Sewing kit (see pages 170–3)
- 12 curtain rings (optional)
- Curtain pole, 20cm (8in) longer than the width of the window, and fixings. Mount according to manufacturer's instructions

The detailed pastoral scenes traditionally depicted in *toile de Jouy* fabric give these curtains an air of timeless elegance and sophistication.

1 To make one curtain panel, use one width each of plain and patterned fabric. For these curtains, both fabrics were 137cm (54in) wide and resulted in finished panels about 134.5cm (53in) wide. If you need wider panels, calculate the number of widths you'll require (see pages 179–80) and join widths or portions of widths (matching patterns) as necessary. Measure the height of your window, according to the desired drop, and add 21.5cm (8½in) to this measurement for the hem and top seam. Measure, mark, and cut a plain and patterned piece of fabric to these dimensions.

2 For the ties measure, mark, and cut 6 strips of fabric, each 85cm (33½in) long by 3.75cm (1½in) wide.

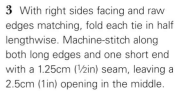

3 With right sides facing and raw edges matching, fold each tie in half lengthwise. Machine-stitch along both long edges and one short end with a 1.25cm (½in) seam, leaving a 2.5cm (1in) opening in the middle.

4 Use the blunt end of a pencil to turn the ties right side out. Hand-sew the other short end closed with slipstitch (see page 174). Press. Repeat for all of the remaining ties.

5 Fold, press, and pin a 10cm (4in) double hem along the bottom edge of the main fabric of each panel. Tack the hems, then hand-sew using hemming stitch (see page 174), or machine-sew using blind hemstitch and a blind hem foot (see page 178). Remove the tacking stitches. Repeat this step for the patterned panels.

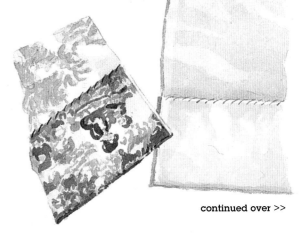

continued over >>

6 Place the plain panel right side up on a work surface. Place the patterned panel on top, right sides facing, raw edges matching. Pin, tack, and machine-stitch 1.25cm (½in) seams around the side and top edges. Turn the panel right side out and press.

A = 7cm (2¾in)
B = 6.5cm (2½in)
C = 1.25cm (½in)
D = 12.75cm (5in)

7 Following the letter guides and red marks in the illustration, measure and mark the positions of the pleats along the top edge of the right side of the plain panel using pins or tailor's chalk.

8 Fold a tie in half crosswise, drape it evenly over the top of a curtain panel at one end (A) and pin it in place. Pin another tie in the same way at the other end of the panel. Pin the remaining ties in place positioning them in the middle of each 12.75cm (5in) gap (D), as shown.

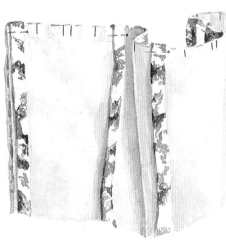

9 Topstitch across the top of the panel 1.25cm (½in) from the top edge, securing the ties and the two layers of fabric in place.

10 Move the ties off the panel, see above. Topstitch along the top edge of the panel, 10cm (4in) below the first line of stitching.

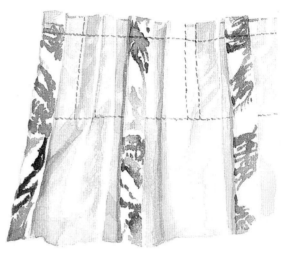

11 To sew the pleats fold the first 6.5cm (2½in) gap (B) in half lengthwise so that the marked lines overlap. Pin and machine-sew a 10cm (4in) vertical line of stitching through all the layers of fabric, starting at the top edge of the panel. Leaving a 1.25cm (½in) gap (C), as indicated, fold, pin, and sew the next pleat (B), in the same manner. Continue for all remaining pleats, until there are five sets of double pleats along the top of the panel. Press the entire panel.

12 Repeat steps 1–12 to make the second curtain panel. Slip the curtain rings onto the rod and tie one pair of ties to each ring. Tie in bows if desired, or attach the ties directly to rod in bows and omit the rings.

Patchwork Curtains

Gathered curtains and a matching valance in classic blue-and-white add cheer to a casual dining room and affirm their country context. The linear pattern of the fringed napkins (checked fabric could also be used) echoes the larger design of the patchwork and contrasts with the curvaceous patterns of circular plates on the wall. Limiting the palette of the soft furnishings to two hues ensures the impact of the medley of patterns does not become overwhelming. For a less casual look, squares of checked or solid coloured fabric, folded under around the edges, could be used.

MATERIALS

- Background fabric (for measuring tips, see pages 179–81)
- Checked fabric or checked napkins, 20cm (8in) square
- Lining fabric
- Pencil pleat curtain tape
- Sewing kit (see pages 170–3)
- Curtain and valance rail and fixings. Mount according to manufacturer's instructions. Position the valance rail 2.5cm (1in) above the curtain rail on brackets that project about 2.5cm (1in) more than those of the curtain rail

Fringed and checked napkins, stitched in a patchwork pattern onto a creamy background fabric, create a patchwork effect on these country cottage-style curtains.

1 To make one curtain panel, use one width of plain fabric. For these curtains, the fabric was 137cm (54in) wide. If you need to make wider panels, calculate the number of widths you'll need and join widths or portions of widths to get the desired width. Measure the height of your window, allowing for the desired drop, and add 19cm (7½in) to this measurement for top and bottom hems. (For measuring windows and joining fabric widths, see pages 179–81.) Measure, mark, and cut a plain panel to these dimensions.

2 If you're using checked fabric rather than napkins, measure, mark, and cut some squares, 22.5cm (9in) of the checked fabric (the number of squares will vary depending on the height and width of your curtain). Fold under and press the raw edges of each square by 1.25cm (½in).

3 Place the background fabric, right side up, on a work surface. If you're using a single width of 137cm (54in) wide fabric, position the first row of squares in a patchwork pattern, 15cm (6in) apart. (The last square should be about 5cm/2in from the other side edge.) Position the next row of squares as shown, tucking the corners or fringes under those above by 1.25cm (½in). Continue tucking the corners of each square under those in the row above, until the pattern is complete. If your fabric width is different, arrange the squares or napkins so they extend evenly from (or fall short of) the side and bottom edges; cut off any excess to align the checked fabric with the curtain edges. Pin and tack the squares in place. Topstitch all around each square about 3mm (⅛in) from the edges; with napkins, topstitch about 3mm (⅛in) from the fringe. Remove the pins and tacking.

4 Turn the panel over so the wrong side faces up. Fold under and press the side edges by 5cm (2in); tack in place. Fold under and press a 6.25cm (2½in) double hem along the bottom edge and machine-topstitch or use blind hemstitch and a blind hem foot (page 178). Or hem by hand using hemming stitch (see page 174). Fold under the top edge by 6.25cm (2½in) and press. Open out the edge and set aside.

5 Measure, mark, and cut a piece of lining fabric equal to the finished dimensions of the curtain panel. Fold in and press 1.25cm (½in) hems along each side and machine-topstitch in place. Fold under and press a 5cm (2in) double hem along the bottom edge and machine-topstitch in place.

6 Place the curtain panel, wrong side up, on a work surface. Place the lining right side up over the curtain. Leaving a 1.25cm (½in) allowance on both sides and a 3.75cm (1½in) allowance along the bottom, pin in place. Machine-topstitch the sides of the lining to the curtain or hand-sew with hemming stitch.

7 Fold down the 6.25cm (2½in) top edge allowance over the lining. Pin the curtain tape over the raw edge 1.25cm (½in) from the folded top edge. Machine-topstitch along the top and bottom edges of the tape, leaving the side edges free.

8 Pull the curtain tape strings to gather the top edge; sew down the short edges. Remove any tacking and trim the strings. Attach curtain hooks and/or rings, spaced about 20cm (8in) apart, to the tape and mount on the rail.

9 Repeat steps 1–8 for the other curtain panel and valance. (Note: Make the cut width of the valance about twice the finished width of the entire treatment; make its finished height about ⅕–⅙ the length of the entire window treatment.)

Sheer Mosquito-net Bed Hanging

Draped in a floaty folded canopy over a bed, sheer fabric lends a delicate, dreamy quality to a bedroom. While mosquito nets have a practical purpose in some countries or beachside homes, bed nets can also be used decoratively to create a romantic, magical ambience. From gauzy muslin or crisp voile to embroidered chiffon, sheers can be layered to float over a four-poster bed or gathered in billowy folds around a hoop and suspended from a hook in the ceiling to add softness and definition to a single bed with a simple headboard or a daybed with no headboard at all.

MATERIALS

- Sheer fabric (striped in this example), such as netting (for measuring tips, see pages 179–81)
- Braid or ribbon trim (optional)
- Cord, 30cm (12in) long, or a ring, 2.5cm (1in) in diameter
- Bed net hoop, 40–60cm (16–24in) in diameter, or a length of clear plastic tubing three times the desired diameter of the hoop and a dowelling stopper
- Cup hook – mounted on the ceiling with fixings appropriate for the weight of the fabric and hoop
- Sewing kit (see pages 170–3)

With their soft feel and see-through lightness, sheer bed nets, either plain or patterned, can add a touch of romance in a guest room.

1 Measure from the bottom of the cup hook to the floor and add 25cm (10in) to get the length dimension. Measure the circumference of the hoop and multiply by 4 to get the width dimension. Measure, mark, and cut a piece of sheer fabric to these dimensions.

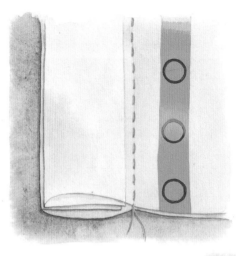

2 If you need to join widths to achieve the desired dimensions (see pages 179–80), neaten the raw edges by joining them by overlocking or with French seams, illustration left (see page 175).

3 Fold and press 6mm (¼in) double hems all around. Measure the diameter of the hoop and divide by 2. Starting from one corner of the top edge, measure and mark a point equal to this dimension along one side edge. Repeat on the opposite side edge. Using a T-square and a ruler, mark a line across the width of the fabric from one of these points to the other.

4 Fold the fabric, right side out, along this line. Measure the circumference of the hoop tubing, divide by 2 and add 6mm (¼in). Measure and mark a line equal to this dimension from the fold and stitch along this line to form the casing for the hoop. Open out the top flap of fabric and place the fabric right side up on a work surface.

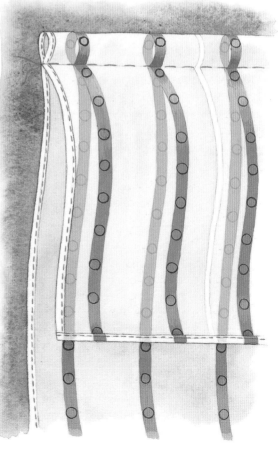

5 Divide the width of the panel by 6. Starting from one short edge, measure and mark points along the top of the hoop casing to segment the width of the fabric into 6 equal portions. Along the top long edge, measure and mark the centre points between each segment. Using the ruler, mark angled lines from the centre points on the top edge to the points on the casing to create triangular shapes, from the top edge to the casing. Starting at one short edge and 1.25cm (½in) above the casing, cut along the angled lines, stopping 1.25cm (½in) from the casing at the bottom edge of each triangle as you go.

6 With the right side of the fabric still up, position and pin the trim on the right side of the fabric along the short sides (length dimension) below the casing, turning under the raw edges of the trim by 1.25cm (½in). Machine-topstitch the trim in place. This step is optional and not shown in the diagram.

7 Place the panel right side up on a work surface. With wrong sides facing, pin the raw edges of the triangles to form a hexagon and machine-sew the triangles together with 1.25cm (½in) seams. Clip into the seams at the base of the triangles along the casing, then finish the seams with flat-fell seams (see page 175).

8 Insert the hoop or tubing into the casing, gathering the fabric as you go. When complete, join the ends of the tube together with a dowelling stopper.

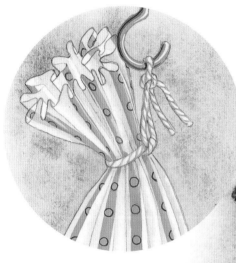

9 Hand-sew the ring to the centre of the top and slip it onto the cup hook. Drape the back of the net behind the head of the bed and part the front of the net over the bed. A simpler way to create the top of the net is to simply gather the flap above the casing in a bunch and tie it together with ribbon or cord and suspend it from the hook without the ring (above).

Cord and Tassel Tiebacks

Tassels and cords come in a vast array of colours, styles, and sizes, and can provide gracious finishing touches to all kinds of window treatments, from traditional formal draperies topped with swags and tails to more contemporary streamlined panels. Simple versions are available at fabric stores and more elaborate and costly hand-made tassels and cords can be purchased through specialist suppliers. But if you wish to coordinate trimmings with fabrics or use unusual yarns, you can easily create them yourself. The following instructions also offer ideas for making simpler or more complex versions of the layered tassel shown here.

MATERIALS

- Thread or yarn in desired colours (fine crochet cotton, wool or linen threads, or embroidery floss or threads are all suitable)
- Pencil
- Cardboard
- Tapestry needle
- Strong cotton sewing thread
- Slim braid
- Sewing kit (see pages 170–3)

This layered and looped tassel and cord has been made with yarns in a variety of complementary hues to create a custom curtain tieback that coordinates with a range of soft furnishings.

1 To make the cord, cut several strands of thread or floss, each three times the desired length of the finished cord. Knot the strands together at each end. Slip one knot over a hook on a door or shelf or tack it to a wall. Insert a pencil between the strands at the other knotted end and stretch them out taut. Twist the pencil around several times until the strands are tightly and evenly twisted along their entire length. (Note: The thickness of the cord will depend on the type of thread, floss, or yarn you are using, as well as the number of strands. Before making your final cord, follow steps 1–3 and experiment with shorter strands until you achieve the desired thickness.)

2 When the strands are tightly twisted, keeping the cord taut, squeeze its middle with your thumb and index finger, then fold it in half and hook the opposite knotted end over the hook. Release your thumb and index finger from the fold – the cord will automatically form into a tighter twist and double in thickness.

3 Tie the two knotted ends together, remove the original two knots, and smooth the cord by hand to even out the twists. (Note: At this point you can make a simple tassel at the folded end of the cord by tying a knot about 9cm (3½in) above the folded end, then trimming off the folded end and fringing out the strands of thread.)

4 To create the looped and layered tassel, cut three pieces of cardboard: one to the desired finished length of the tassel, the second about 6–12mm (¼–½in) shorter, and the third 6–12mm (¼–½in) shorter than the second. Wind thread, floss, or yarn several times around the three pieces of cardboard. The thicker your thread or yarn and the more turns you make, the fuller the tassel will be. If you are using more than one colour and want to make several identical tassels, note the pattern of the threads and wind subsequent tassels in the same way. Using a tapestry needle and strong sewing thread, backstitch (see page 173) along the top edge of the threads on each piece of cardboard, making sure all strands are linked together as one fringe. (Note: To make a simple tassel without layers, follow these instructions, but use just one piece of cardboard, and cut the bottom of the strands at the lower end of the cardboard after the top has been backstitched into a fringe.)

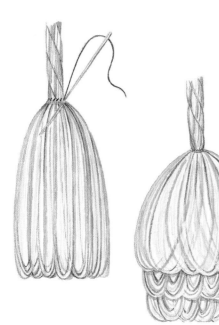

5 Slip the longest looped fringe off the cardboard and wrap it around the knotted end of the cord, securing it to the cord by hand stitching through the backstitched edge and through the concealed knot at the end of the cord. Slip the second longest fringe off the cardboard and wrap it around the cord on top of the first; secure in place in the same way. Repeat this process with the last fringe.

6 Tie a piece of strong thread around the tassel, just below the hidden knot on the cord, to create a rounded head. Finish the tassel by wrapping a length of slim braid or wool, such as a strong boucle wool, around the tassel over this thread, and glue or tie in place.

7 You can create a more ornate head by adorning the area between the cord and the braid with embroidered stitches. Wrap a thread around the cord where it meets the top of the tassel and secure in place. Starting at this ring of thread, hand-sew blanket stitches (see page 174) from the ring into the tassel below, about 6mm (¼in) from the cord. Continue making rows of blanket stitches in this manner until you reach the braid binding. Or, if you're a skilled embroiderer, experiment with other stitches, or use beads or other contrasting threads, to enhance the design.

right A pair of triple-layered fringed tassels with structured heads provides an elegant tieback for a traditional curtain trimmed with a contrasting brush tassel fringe.

Four-poster-bed Hangings

During the 13th century, when bed canopies first appeared, lords or ladies who lived in stone castles often shared their sleeping areas with servants or attendants. And so, beds with canopies not only signified status, but also served as a means to provide warmth and privacy. Today, the rich tapestries that adorned the bedposts of early beds are replaced with lighter fabrics, which cocoon the bed, creating a sense of luxury and protecting against draughts. This canopy with its contrasting lining fabric and slender loops and ties, is relatively easy to make and is also simple to remove for cleaning.

MATERIALS

- Floral fabric (for measuring tips, see pages 179–81). You will need enough to make four side panels, two panels for the foot of the bed, one panel for the head of the bead and one panel for the top canopy
- Check fabric – for quantities see floral fabric
- Contrasting fabric – about 5m (5½yd) for edging, loops, and ties
- Sewing kit (see pages 170–3)

Contrasting fabrics and tie, loop, and edging detailing, create a sense of grandeur and disguise the fact that these hangings are very simple.

1 Measure the inside height and width of the side of the bed frame for the side panels (A). Measure the height and width of the foot of the bed frame for the foot panels (B); double the width of (B) to get the width measurement of the head panel (C), which will have the same height measurement as (A) and (B). Add 2.5cm (1in) to each dimension. Measure, mark, and cut four pieces from each of the two mains fabrics to the dimensions of panel (A); two pieces from each fabric to the dimensions of panel (B); and one piece from each fabric to the dimensions of panel (C). If you need to make panels wider than the width of the fabric, calculate the number of widths you'll need (see page 180) and join widths or portions of widths (matching patterns as necessary) to get the desired size.

2 Use the width of panel (A) and the width of panel (B) to get the size of the top canopy panel. Add 5cm (2in) to each dimension. Measure, mark, and cut one piece from each of the two main fabrics to these dimensions.

3 To make the edging for the panels: measure, mark, and cut enough pieces of contrasting fabric, 5cm (2in) wide and on the bias, to surround the perimeter of each panel. Join the strips with 6mm (¼in) seams on the diagonal (see pages 176–7) to create one long piece of edging. Fold the strip in half lengthwise, right sides out; press.

4 To make the loops for each panel: measure, mark, and cut strips of contrasting fabric, 4.5 by 15–20cm (1¾ by 6–8in) – each loop should be 5cm (2in) longer than the diameter of the top rail). Cut enough strips so that there will be one at each end and several others evenly spaced along each edge about 15cm (6in) apart. Fold each strip in half lengthwise, right sides out; press. Fold in the long raw edges by 6mm (¼in); press. Machine-topstitch to close the edges.

5 To make the ties for the top canopy: measure, mark, and cut 18 pieces of contrasting fabric, each measuring 3.75 by 70cm (28 by 1½in). Fold each strip in half lengthwise, right sides out; press. Fold in the long and short raw edges by 6mm (¼in); press. Machine-topstitch to close the edges.

6 To make the top canopy: place the floral fabric, right side up on a flat surface. Place the contrasting edging around the perimeter, raw edges matching, and pin. Fold each tie in half crosswise. Slip the fold of each tie over the raw sides of the edging about 3.75cm (1½in) from each end around all four sides. Evenly space two ties between the end ties on the short sides, and three ties between the end ties on the long sides. Pin and tack in place.

7 Place the checked fabric on top of the floral fabric, right sides facing, raw edges matching. Pin and tack around all four sides. Machine-stitch all around with 1.25cm (½in) seams, leaving a 20cm (8in) opening along one short side. Turn the panel right side out. Press; close the opening with a row of slipstitches (see pages 173–4).

8 To make the hangings: place the floral fabric, right side up on a flat surface. Place the contrasting edging around the perimeter, raw edges matching; pin. Fold each loop in half crosswise. With the raw edges of the loop aligning with the edging, pin one loop 3.75cm (1½in) from each end of one short side and evenly space the remaining loops between. Tack the edging and the loops to the fabric.

9 Place the checked fabric on top of the floral fabric, right sides facing, raw edges matching. Pin and tack around all four sides. Machine-stitch all around with 1.25cm (½in) seams, leaving a 20cm (8in) opening along the bottom side. Turn the panel right side out. Press; close the opening with a row of slipstitches. Repeat steps 8–9 for all other hangings.

10 Dismantle the top rails of the bed frame; slip the rails through the loops of the hangings and reattach the rail. Tie the top canopy to the top of the bed frame spacing the ties between the loops.

opposite page Gracefully draped over a four-poster caopy bed, white cotton sheer bed curtains are casually raised with matching ties on the sides and foot of the bed like modified London blinds.

Corona Canopy

Like four-poster-bed hangings, corona canopies are no longer required for privacy and protection from draughts, but can still be valued for bringing warmth and an air of luxury to bedroom settings. This corona is made using an oval board (though circular is equally effective), covered with fabric and concealed by a fabric crown. Half-coronas, which are mounted on the wall, give the same effect but require less fabric.

MATERIALS

- Main decorative fabric (for measuring tips see pages 179–81)
- Contrasting decorative fabric for lining
- Curtain heading tape and curtain hooks
- Braid
- Buckram
- Hook-and-loop (touch-and-close) tape
- Staple gun and staples
- Fabric adhesive
- Sewing kit (see pages 170–3)

To make and fix the corona, you will need:

- Medium-density fibreboard (MDF) or plywood, 1.25–2cm (½–¾in) thick
- Coping saw or jigsaw, sandpaper, screw eyes, screws, hooks and eyes; for half-corona also 2 L-shaped brackets

This vibrant *lit a la Turque* canopy is suspended from a fabric-covered oval-shaped board that is mounted to the ceiling.

1 Choose either an oval or circular shape for your corona. Determine the size of the corona based on the bed it will top. For a single bed its diameter should be about 50cm (20in), for a double or queen-size bed about 60cm (24in). For a wall-mounted half-corona, the straight, back edge should be one of these dimensions. Using a compass or other circular template, draw a circular shape on the MDF or plywood. Or, if you don't have a compass, tie a piece of string around a pencil and tape it to the centre of the plywood so the string measures ½ the desired diameter. Hold the pencil straight up with the pencil point on the board. Stretching the string taut, pull the pencil around in a circle or semi-circle to draw the shape on the board. Cut out the shape with a coping saw or jigsaw and smooth the edges with sandpaper.

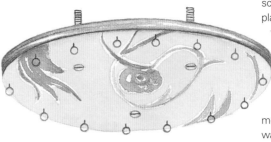

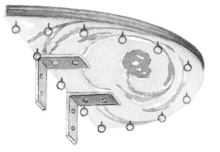

2 Place the main decorative fabric face down on a work surface. Place the shaped board on the fabric and trace around it, adding 1.25cm (½in) all around. Cut out the shape from the fabric. Fold under and press the allowance to the wrong side of the circle, clipping as needed to lay flat. Apply fabric adhesive around the allowance, then place the shaped board on top to secure it to the fabric.

3 Insert about 35–45 screw eyes into the fabric side of the board, about 1.25cm (½in) from the perimeter and evenly spaced about 5–7.5cm (2–3in) apart.

4 To mount the corona to the ceiling, drill three starter holes through the board about 5cm (2in) from the perimeter in a triangle pattern. Hold the board up to the ceiling and mark the positions of the screw holes with a pencil. Remove the board, and using a drill bit slightly smaller than the diameter of the wall anchor, drill holes into the ceiling at the marks. Insert the wall anchors into the holes, using a hammer to align the anchors flush with the ceiling. Insert the screws into the corona board and attach it to the ceiling, fabric side facing out. (Note: With a half-corona, attach the L-shaped brackets to the back edge of the board with 1.25cm (½in) screws, then fix it to the wall in the desired place, using wall anchors as described above. If you don't want the brackets to show, apply the fabric after you've attached the brackets to the board.)

5 To determine length of your curtain, measure from the corona (on the ceiling or wall) out to the side of the bed beneath it and then to the floor. Add 17.5cm (7in) to this dimension for the heading and hem. For a single bed, you'll need about 4½ widths of 137cm (54in) wide fabric – 1½ widths for each side curtain and 1½ widths for the back curtain. For a double bed, you'll need about 6 total widths – 2 widths for each side curtain and 2 widths for the back curtain.

6 Measure, mark, and cut all the curtain panels, joining the widths with 1.25cm (½in) seams and matching patterns if necessary (see page 180). Repeat for the lining fabric, this time adding 7.5cm (3in), rather than 17.5cm (7in) to the length for heading and hem, and trimming 5cm (2in) from one side edge of the joined widths of each side curtain. Press open the seams. Cut off the selvages or clip into the allowance to keep the fabric from pulling. (Note: If you're using a half-corona, you'll need only lining fabric for the back curtain since it will lie flat against the wall.)

9 Turn the curtain right side out. Press one side seam so there is a 5cm (2in) border of main fabric showing on the leading edge of the lining fabric side. Press the other side flat so the seam line is flush with the curtain edge (so neither fabric shows on the other side).

10 Before hemming the side curtains, mitre the corners of the leading edge. Fold up and press a 6.25cm (2½in) double hem along the bottom edge of the main fabric. Place a pin along the leading edge where the bottom edge will finish (A); unfold half of the hem and place a pin at the fold of the hem where the leading edge finishes (B). Unfold the leading edge completely and fold in the corner between the pin marks on the diagonal (C). Then refold the remainder of the hem and fold in the leading edge to mitre the corner (D). Tack the hem.

7 To make the side curtains, place the lining fabric over the main fabric on a work surface, right sides facing and top raw edges aligned. Pin the raw side edges together (the main fabric panels will be 5cm/2in wider than the lining panels). Starting 2.5cm (1in) below the top edge and stopping 5cm (2in) above the bottom edge of the lining fabric, machine-stitch the side edges with 1.25cm (½in) seams (the bottom raw edge will extend 11.25cm/4½in beyond the bottom edge of the lining fabric).

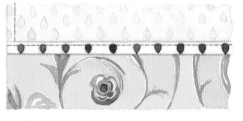

8 On the lining fabric, fold under and press a 2.5cm (1in) double hem towards the wrong side of the lining fabric and machine-topstitch to close the hem.

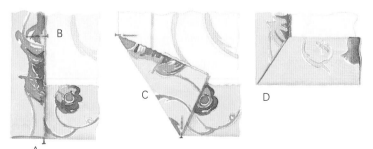

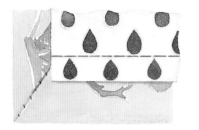

11 Close the mitred folds with slipstitch (see pages 173–4) and finish the hem of the main fabric by machine with blind hemstitch and a blind-hem foot (see page 178), or by hand with hemming stitch (see page 174). Remove the tacking stitches.

12 Fold over the top edge of the main fabric by 2.5cm (1in) to the wrong side; press. Fold the top edge of the lining fabric over the top edge of the main fabric by 2.5cm (1in); press.

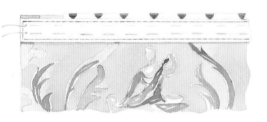

13 Place the heading tape over the raw edge of the lining fabric 6mm (¼in) from the top edge; pin. Turn under the short ends of the tape by 6mm (¼in) cm and pin in place, making sure the drawing cords are free. Machine-topstitch around the top, bottom and side edges of the tape, without sewing over the cords.

14 To make the back curtain, place the joined widths of the main and lining panels, right sides facing and raw edges matching, on a work surface. Pin, then machine-stitch the side edges together with 1.25cm (½in) seams. Turn the panel right side

out and press the side edges flat. Note: If you are making the half-corona and not using main fabric for the back curtain, fold over, press, and machine-stitch the side edges on the lining fabric with a 2.5cm (1in) double hem towards the wrong side.

15 Fold under, press, and machine-stitch a 2.5cm (1in) double hem along the bottom of the lining fabric towards the wrong side. Fold under and press a 6.25cm (2½in) double hem along the bottom of the main fabric towards the wrong side; pin in place. Sew the hems by hand with hemming stitch, or by machine with blind hemstitch and a blind-hem foot. Fold over the top edge of the main fabric by 2.5cm (1in) to the wrong side; press. Fold the top edge of the lining fabric over the top edge of the main fabric by 2.5cm (1in); press. Attach the heading tape as described for the side curtains, step 13.

16 When hung, the finished curtains should appear as a single curtain. To achieve this effect, hand-sew hooks at evenly spaced intervals along the backs of the side edges; hand-sew eyes to align with these hooks along the side edges of the back curtain, so that they may be held together from the corona down to bed height.

17 Draw the strings of the header tape on each curtain until together they fit the circumference of the corona and tie off or sew the strings in place. Insert curtain hooks, equal to the number of screw eyes in the board, into the header tape at evenly spaced intervals and attach to the screw eyes.

18 To make the pleated pelmet, measure, mark, and cut a piece of main fabric, three times the circumference of the corona board in length by 17.5cm (7in) wide. Measure, mark, and cut a piece of lining fabric equal in length to the circumference of the corona board plus 2.5cm (1in) by 17.5cm (7in) wide. (Note: For the half-corona, the length of the lining fabric should equal the length of the front curved edge of the board plus 2.5cm/1in.) Measure, mark, and cut a piece of buckram to the same size as the lining fabric strip, less 2.5cm (1in) all around.

19 Fold and pin pleats, approximately 3.75–5cm (1½–2in) deep, all around the strip of main fabric until the fabric fits around the perimeter of the corona board and the short ends overlap by 1.25cm (½in). Press, then machine-topstitch 6mm (¼in) from the raw top and bottom edges to secure the pleats in place. Centre the buckram over the wrong side of the pleated pelmet, and attach using herringbone stitch (see page 174). Fold over and press the pleated seam allowances and short ends of the pelmet to the wrong side of the fabric, over the buckram, and tack in place.

20 On the right side of the pleated pelmet, place and pin the braid along the top and bottom edges and machine- or hand-sew in place through all thicknesses of the fabric.

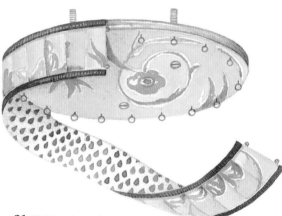

21 Fold under and press the seam allowance of the lining strip to the wrong side. Hand-sew it to the pleated pelmet using slipstitch. Cut a length of hook-and-loop (touch-and-close) tape equal to the circumference of the corona board (or the front side, for a half-corona). Separate the two sides of the hook-and-loop tape, wrap one side around the perimeter of the corona and staple in place. Hand- or machine-sew the other piece along the top inside edge of the pelmet. Hand-sew hooks and eyes to the short edges of the pelmet; attach the two sides of the tape and close the hooks and eyes to secure the pelmet in place.

opposite page A corona bed canopy in soft cream is enlivened by a striped fabric cut on the bias. The spotted curtains are edged to match.

pelmets

Whether used alone as a single decorative element or in tandem with curtains or blinds, a top treatment gives character to a window, perhaps by adding a subtle finish or by making a dramatic statement. From valances, pelmets, and flags to cornices, lambrequins, and swags, options for top treatments are many, and the style choices within each category are limitless. Picture the quiet romance of a soft shirred valance with a ruffled top in a country guest room, the classic elegance of waterfall swags and tails over floor-length curtains in a townhouse living room, and the understated charm of a gingham box-pleated pelmet over a sunny kitchen window. Soft or structured, simple or complex, streamlined and modern, or shaped and whimsical, these window dressings offer great opportunities for creative expression: a selection of key examples are described in the projects on pages 74–83. And they can solve problems – increasing the perceived size of a small window or concealing less-than-appealing window frames – too.

making it

AT THE TOP

With an infinite array of top treatments to choose from, settling on a style that's right for your window may seem daunting. But honing in on the architectural character of your room, along with the decorative ambience you aim to achieve, is the best way to start narrowing your options.

above Draped over small wooden tiebacks, a cotton muslin swag in a buttery hue lends a touch of formality over gingham blinds in a country kitchen.
right Bunched at each corner with a knotted rosette, a relaxed swag and tails provides a soft finishing touch over full-length curtains set inside a window-seat niche and made of the same sunny taffeta fabric.
far right Edged with a lively trim, this flat valance provides a crisp finish to floor-length curtains in a matching fabric.

Choosing a Style that Works

Unless you live in house that's quite grand with large rooms and imposing windows, an intricately shaped and strongly structured lambrequin (see page 71) – or its longer-legged cousin, a catonniere – is probably more than your windows can take. On the other hand, a simpler lambrequin with understated scrolls and a simple arch covered with a cheerful fabric could be just what a large window in an undistinguished room needs to introduce a note of architectural impact (see pages 78–9). By the same token, the clean lines of a structured cornice would work beautifully in a modern space, but a box-pleated valance (see pages 74–5) could just as easily provide a streamlined finish while introducing a touch of softness.

Unusually shaped windows, such as arches or bays, or those that are deeply recessed will play a leading role in directing your choices. And top treatments also offer the perfect chance to mask architectural shortcomings – such as a too-small window – and fix design problems, such as blocking light from over-size windows or giving a more comfortable scale to tall windows.

Consider, too, whether you want a pelmet or lambrequin to stand alone and serve as an understated finishing touch for your window, or to be part of the whole, complementing a layered treatment, which may include curtains and sheers or soft blinds or roller blinds. Whichever style you choose, it should blend with the character and colours of other hard and soft furnishings in the room, as well as any window dressings it may be paired with.

Types of Treatments

Basically, window top treatments fall into two categories: soft, including valances, pelmets, and swags, and hard, including cornices and lambrequins. Although the dominant aspects of the soft variety are the fabric and draping, soft top treatments are always mounted on a hard rod or mounting board, which helps to give them definition. And although the salient features of the hard variety are structured and sometimes intricately shaped and tooled, they are often padded and covered with fabric, which can even be shirred, to lend them a touch of softness.

above This shaped valance is trimmed with contrasting cord and adorned at the centre with a starfish, which echoes the boss, or holdback, over which the shell-trimmed curtain is loosely draped.
left Mounted on a tension rod, a plain valance, enlivened with a zigzag edge, provides a playful touch over simple white cotton curtains in this airy room.

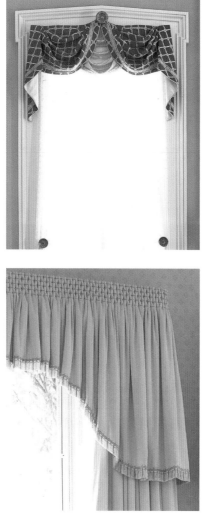

top left Shirred and adorned with lavish rosettes, a glorious Austrian valance tops puddling bedroom curtains with layers of dreamy softness.
top centre Mounted over undercurtains, this formal swag with pleated tails makes a strong statement to match the richly moulded window frame.
bottom centre In the bedroom of an English manor house, floor-length curtains are topped with gathered valances that have hand-sewn smocked headings.
top right A *toile de Jouy* valance with a shaped edge brightens the window in front of a quiet reading nook.

Valances

A valance is a border of fabric running along the top of a window. Valances can be used alone or in conjunction with blinds, full-length curtains, or shutters. Some imitate the qualities of swags and are flanked by cascades – trims, often of lace, arranged in loose waves – or punctuated with frills of lace, known as jabots. Others can be arched with contrasting festoons.

While many are soft and informal, valances can also be carefully structured with rows of rhythmic pleats, attached to a projecting mounting board, or they can hang gracefully from rods in sweeping lines; there are those that have a peaked or an arched formation and drape from decorative ceiling hooks. They can

be as simple as a straight flat panel with kick pleats at the corners, or complex and layered with two types of fabric and ruffled trim.

Flags, banners, or scarves are pendant, draped, or shaped pieces of fabric that may flank a valance mounted on a pole, or provide a flourish at the top of stationary panels. They are suspended from poles or hooks by loops, hooks, or bows at maybe two, three, or four points along their top hem.

Pelmets

A pelmet is basically a valance but with the fabric stiffened, and sometimes interlined. It usually sports a distinctly detailed lower edge, such as zigzags (see pages 80–3), scallops, or crenellated shapes, which are often themselves highlighted with decorative trim or tassels. Like valances, pelmets can be paired with tails, cascades, and jabots. They can also incorporate layers of stiffened fabric to create a more three-dimensional effect.

Swags

Swags are wedge-shaped cuts of fabric with rounded edges that are draped in soft pleats and often flanked by tails, jabots, or cascades (see pages 76–7). Typically, swags are most suited to traditional formal settings and are paired with curtains. But a gathered swag with a ruffled top or a switchback swag draped casually over a pole would work in more relaxed rooms, too. A narrow window might be topped with a single swag, but wider windows are often topped with two, three, or even five swags; these may be draped in a classic centre swag arrangement or be overlapped to the left or to the right or in other constructions. They are often trimmed with bullion fringe or other fringes or tassels.

above Suspended from three rosettes, a deep double swag provides an elegant finish over abundant curtains. A pair of tassels accent the centre of the swag.
far left A single swag flanked by long pleated tails in a striped fabric gives a formal air to a hall window.
left The folds of these carefully arranged pleated tails are highlighted by a lining fabric that picks up the colour of the stripes on the main fabric.

above A shirred and shaped valance provides a soft, rich finishing touch above curtains in a matching fabric.
top right Mounted over simple curtains, a scalloped valance in an oversize check fabric gives this bedroom graphic punch.
right A white-painted, moulded cornice provides a crisp, classic finish above a window flanked by basic floor-length curtains.
far right A red-painted cornice warms this window and increases its perceived height. Its scalloped lower edge echoes the ruffled *toile de Jouy* valance mounted beneath it.

Cornices

A cornice is a hard top-treatment used alone or in combination with curtains, blinds, or layers. It can be made of architectural moulding, painted wood panels, metal, or medium-density fibreboard (MDF) covered with fabric.

Some cornices are flat boxes finished with fretwork and topped by moulding. Others are padded, upholstered, and adorned with nail heads. They can be covered with shirred fabric to give them softness, or shaped like a pagoda and embellished with trimmings such as gimp or tassels for a sense of drama or whimsy. Although they can be complex and lavish for formal settings, they can also be streamlined for contemporary rooms, softened for romantic spaces, or simplified for casual environments.

Lambrequins and Catonnieres

A lambrequin is structured like a cornice but always has extended sides, or legs, which stretch down to frame more of the window. A catonniere is a lambrequin with legs that stretch to the floor. Like cornices, lambrequins and catonnieres can be painted or papered, or padded and upholstered. They can be used alone or with under treatments, such as blinds, sheers, or curtains.

Typically made with plywood or medium-density fibreboard (MDF), their interior edges are often elaborately cut and shaped with scrolls, scallops, peaks, or arches. And they are often embellished with trims, ribbons, tassels, or borders to accentuate their form. They are used to add architectural character, unify a set of closely positioned windows, or alter the overall shape of a window. In general, they are most suited to traditional spaces.

Practical Considerations

All top treatments are supported by a pole, board, or other structured and shaped foundation, mounted on brackets. If you plan to use a pole in combination with curtains,

choose a double style, which will allow you to hang both from the same bracket.

Where a top treatment is mounted to boards, it should be attached to the wall with L-shaped brackets. When used in combination with other soft furnishings, such as curtain panels, whether operable or stationary, the boards need to be wide enough to clear everything below, and allow breathing room for the fabric to drape gracefully.

Remember to purchase sufficient fabric to be able to cover the returns on any mounting boards. If these can be seen from above or below, they should also be lined so they look finished from these directions, too. Finally, always choose appropriate wall anchors and enough brackets to support the weight of any top treatment in your wall.

top Box-shaped cornices link a pair of windows with a set of double doors. The subtle large-scale check fabric echoes the linear character of the cornices.
above Decorated with braid and tassels and mounted beneath an elaborate cornice, this intricately cut, fabric-covered lambrequin provides a fancy finishing touch.

Pelmet styles and types

1–2 Shaped Hem
Teamed with matching curtains, a valance with a handkerchief hem brings a zesty touch to a window. Soften the playful effect by using a sheer fabric and gathering it along the top to form graceful folds *(left)*. Or, make a bold statement with a bright, striped fabric and trim the zigzag edge of a pelmet with braid and tassels *(right)*.

SEE **ZIGZAG PELMET, PAGES 80–3**

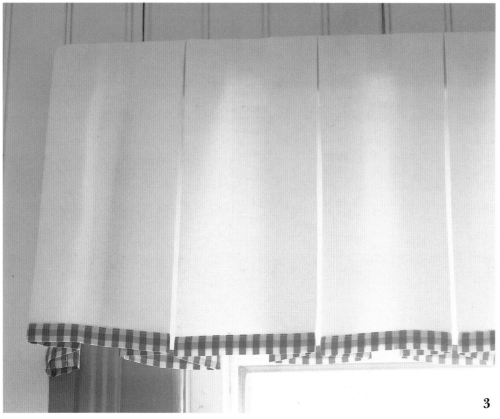

3 Trimmed Box Pleat
A cotton or linen valance with crisp box pleats provides a simple yet polished dressing for windows in traditional or contemporary rooms. Use this classic treatment alone or over a roller blind for light control and privacy. Finish the hem with a gingham trim for a casual touch, or a plain-coloured fabric for a more tailored look.

SEE **UNLINED BOX-PLEATED VALANCE, PAGES 74–5**

4 Scrolled Edge
Edged with piping and stretched taut over an arched or scroll-cut board, a pretty fabric becomes a dramatic lambrequin *(right)*. Placed in front of a tailored Roman blind or softly pleated panels in a matching fabric, fabric-covered pelmets can make a window the focal point of a room.

SEE **FABRIC-COVERED LAMBREQUIN, PAGES 78–9**

5 Scalloped Edge

It is easy to add a whimsical note to a flat valance. This scalloped edge works well in this room where the valance is shaped in a curve to echoe the half-moon lines of the scallops. Finish the semi-circular edges with seam-binding or contrasting fabric cut on the bias.

6 Shirred Ruffle

Shirring tape sewn to the top edge gives a plain valance flirty fullness. Before pulling the shirring cords, topstitch a slim grosgrain or satin ribbon in a contrasting colour along the bottom edge to accent the ruffles. Pair the valance with short or full-length panels in a complementary print.

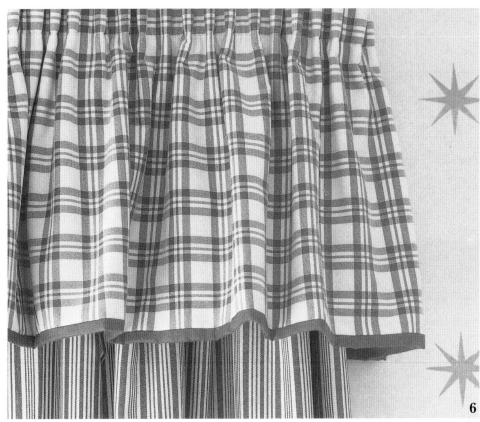

Unlined Box-pleated Valance

This tailored box-pleated linen valance adds flair while still allowing sunlight to pour into the room and without blocking the view. Set off by a built-in banquette with cushions in contrasting floral fabric, the simple valance brings a touch of requisite softness to the window. The charming checked trim matches the window moulding and links the valance with the accent cushions, while allowing the colourful floral fabric and flowers in the window box to stand out.

MATERIALS

- Main fabric (for measuring tips, see pages 179–81)
- Contrasting fabric for trim
- Staple gun and staples
- Sewing kit (see pages 170–3)

To make the valance frame, you will need:

- Medium-density fibreboard (MDF) or plywood, 1.25–2cm (½–¾in) thick by 5–15cm (2–6in) wide
- L-shaped brackets and appropriate screws
- Tools and fixings for cutting the board and attaching the valance frame to the wall

Trimmed with a slender band of gingham fabric, a box-pleated linen valance provides an understated finishing touch to this window.

1 Measure the outside width of the window frame, add 2.5–5cm (1–2in), and cut a length of board to this dimension. Divide the length of the board by 8 to determine the face width of each pleat across the front.

2 To determine the cut length of the valance add 142cm (56in) to the length of the board, plus twice the depth of the return. To get the cut height of the valance, measure from the planned position on the wall of the top of the board to the windowsill, divide this measurement by 5, then add 5cm (2in). Measure, mark, and cut a piece of main fabric to these dimensions. Machine-stitch the top edge of the valance with overcast stitch using an edging or overcast foot (see page 178).

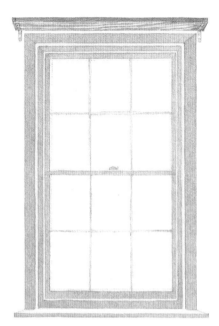

3 Measure, mark, and cut a strip of contrasting fabric equal to the cut length of the valance fabric and 7.5cm (3in) wide. Fold and press this strip in half lengthwise. Fold in and press the long raw edges of the strip 1.25cm (½in) to the wrong side. Open out the folds.

4 Place the contrasting trim on top of the valance fabric, right sides facing, with one long raw edge positioned 1.25cm (½in) from the raw bottom edge of the valance. Pin in place and machine-stitch the contrasting trim to the valance fabric along the seam allowance fold line; if you wish, you can use an edge/quilting guide (see page 178) along the centre fold line to keep the trim straight.

5 Fold the rest of the trim around the valance so the centre fold aligns with the bottom raw edge. Fold in the seam allowance along the back of the valance and hand-sew with hemming stitch (see page 174) to close the trim and encase the bottom edge of the valance (right). Or, to machine-sew the back edge of the trim in place, press and pin the back folded edge slightly higher than the front folded edge then stitch in the ditch (stitch along the seam) of the front sewn edge of the trim.

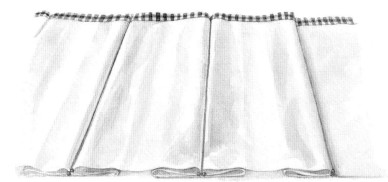

7 With the fabric still facing up, bring the second pin to meet the first; centre and press the fabric beneath the pins to form 7.5cm (3in) box pleats. Bring the fourth pin to meet the third; centre and press the fabric beneath the pins to form the next 7.5cm (3in) box pleat. Continue until all the pleats are folded and pressed. Pin the pleats in place. Machine-tack along the length of the valance 2.5cm (1in) from the top edge to secure the pleats in place. Fold over the top edge of the valance by 5cm (2in) towards the wrong side of the fabric and press.

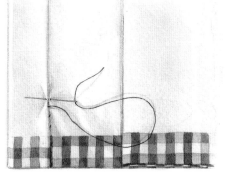

8 Fold under and press 1.25cm (½in) double hems along both short edges of the valance. Close the hems by hand using hemming stitch, or by machine using blind hem stitch and blind hem foot (see page 178).

9 Position the folded edge of the valance along the front of the board, making sure the first and last pleats fold neatly around the corners and that the ends cover the returns, adjusting if necessary. Staple the top of the pelmet to the board, neatly folding under and mitring the fabric at the corners.

10 Screw the L-shaped brackets into the underside of the board. Hold the board over the window and mark the positions of the screw holes. Using appropriate fixings and tools, attach the valance board to the wall.

6 Place the valance fabric face up on a work surface. Starting at one short end, measure the depth of the return, add 2.5cm (1in). Place a pin here at the top edge of the fabric to mark the position of the first pleat. Measure 15cm (6in) to mark the position of the other side of this pleat. Then measure the width of the face of the pleat (as determined in step 1) and place a pin at this position. Continue measuring 15cm (6in), then the face width of the pleat, then 15cm (6in), then the face width of the pleat, marking with pins until all of the pleats are marked. The last pleat should be positioned at a distance equal to the return plus 2.5cm (1in) from the other end.

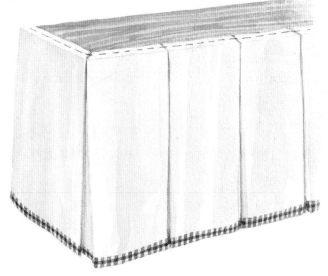

Classic Swags and Tails

Gracious swags and cascading tails, especially when paired with luxurious puddled curtains, enrich windows with a sense of formality and tradition. The key to success is proper proportion: to create a pleasing balance, the deepest point of the swag should be about one fifth of the measurement from the top of the entire treatment to the floor. For very tall windows, it can be as deep as a quarter of the total height. Tails should run from one third to two thirds of the overall drop. For pleated tails like the ones shown here, the backsides of the folds will be visible from the front, so line them with the main fabric or a contrasting decorative fabric. Deep bullion fringe or braid and tassel trims (see pages 54–5) add a luxurious finishing touch.

MATERIALS

- Main fabric (for measuring tips, see pages 179–81)
- Lining fabric
- Light chain or heavy cord
- Bullion fringe
- Flanged rope cord
- Tassels on cords
- Cotton tape, 5cm (2in) wide
- Masking tape
- Tacks
- Staple gun and staples
- Sewing kit (see pages 170–3)

To make the pelmet frame you will need:
- Board or lath 2.5cm (1in) thick by 10–15cm (4–6in) wide
- L-shaped brackets and screws
- Tools and fixings for cutting the board and attaching the pelmet to the wall

right Silk curtains topped with generous swags and pleated tails (one side shown only) trimmed with a deep bullion fringe lend an air of opulence to windows.

1 Determine the total finished width of the swag and tails as an ensemble – it should be about 2.5–5cm (1–2in) larger than the curtain rail beneath it (see pages 179–81) – and cut the board or lath to this width. Divide the length of the board in ½ and mark its centre point at the front edge. Divide ½ the length of the board by 5 and, starting from the side edge, measure and mark points equal to this distance on the front edge of the board, denoting the inner edge of each tail and the position of the swags. The tails should occupy ¹⁄₁₀ of the board each, plus the width of the return and the swags should occupy the centre ⅘ of the board (⅖ each).

3 To make a pattern for the swag, measure and cut a piece of pattern paper equal to twice the depth of the swag by the bottom width of the swag. Fold the paper in half crosswise. On a short side, mark a point about 5cm (2in) from the bottom edge (A). Starting from the folded edge, draw a curve towards (A). Flip the paper over and trace the line to complete the curve on the other side. Divide the length of the

2 Determine the finished depth of the swag at its deepest point (it should be ¼–⅕ of the height between the floor and the top of the mounted position of the board). Tack a light chain or heavy cord from one end point of the swag to the other on the board, allowing it to drape to the finished depth in the middle. Mark or cut the chain or cord just past the tacks and remove it from the board. The length of the marked or cut cord or chain is the finished width of the bottom of the swag.

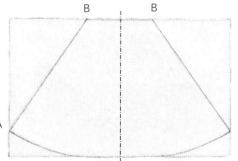

pattern into 3 and mark these points along the top of the pattern (B). Using the ruler, mark angled lines from each end of the curved line to the marks (B) on either side of the fold to create a wedge-shape pattern, as shown.

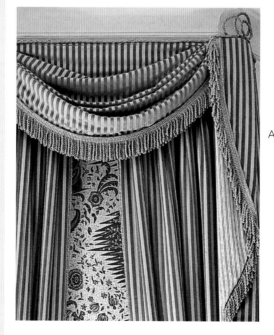

4 Pin the pattern to the main fabric, and cut out, adding a 1.25cm (½in) seam allowance along the curved edge and 5cm (2in) to all other sides before cutting. Repeat for the lining fabric. (Note: With a solid colour or non-directional patterned or woven fabric, cutting your swag on the bias will allow it to drape more easily. Cutting on the bias is not possible with printed or woven fabrics with directional patterns.)

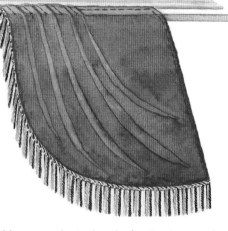

5 To get the cut length of the tail add 7.5cm (3in) to the finished length of the tails at their longest point. (The tails in this treatment are about ⅔ the height from the top of the mounted swag to the floor.) To get the cut width of the tail, triple the finished width of the tail as marked on the board, add the finished width to this figure, plus the width of the return, plus 2.5cm (1in) for seam allowances.

6 Make a pattern for the tails: measure and cut a piece of pattern paper the cut width and length of the tail. On one long side, mark a point ¼ of the way from the top (C). On the top short side, mark a point 2.5cm (1in) from the edge (D). Using a ruler, draw a line from (C) to (D), and draw another line from (C) to the bottom corner of the opposite long side (E). The shorter angled line at the top allows the tail folds to taper. Cut out the pattern, pin it to the fabric, and cut out, adding a 1.25cm (½in) seam allowance all around. Cut out a piece of lining fabric. Flip the pattern and cut out the fabric for the other tail.

7 To make each swag, place the main fabric over the lining, right sides facing, raw edges matching. Pin, tack, and machine-stitch the curved edges together with 1.25cm (½in) seams. Clip into the allowance, turn right side out, and press. Tack the lining and main fabric together along the other raw edges. Hand-sew the bullion fringe to the curved edge.

8 Measure and cut a length of cotton tape equal to the finished width of each swag plus 5cm (2in), lay it out flat and tape the ends to a work surface. Mark the centre of the swag on the tape, then pin the centre of the swag to the tape. Working from one of the angled sides of the swag, fold in 4 or 5 rough pleats and pin to the tape, leaving about 2.5cm (1in) of the tape free at the end for turning. (Position the first pleat to overlap the top edge of the unpleated centre of the swag.) Repeat on the other angled side. Machine-stitch across the folds and through the tape to secure them. Turn in the ends of the tape, then machine-sew a second row of stitches 1.25cm (½in) from the first over the folds and through the tape to doubly secure them. Repeat to create the other swag. Staple the top edge of each swag to the top of the board.

9 To make each tail, place the main fabric and lining pieces together, with right sides facing and raw edges matching. Pin, tack, and machine-sew the pieces together along the sides and sloping bottom edge with 2.5cm (1in) seams. Clip the bottom corners of the seam allowance. Turn the tails right side out and press the seams. Tack the main fabric and lining together along the top edge. Hand-sew the bullion fringe to the short sides and angled bottom edges of both tails.

10 Measure and cut a length of cotton tape equal to the finished width of the tail, including the return, plus 5cm (2in) for turning under. Tape it to a work surface. Mark off the length of the return on the tape. Starting at the short edge of the tail, form 3½ pleats, each equal to the front finished width of the tail, leaving the long edge of the last pleat free to wrap around the return. Pin the pleated tail to the tape and machine-stitch over the folds through the tape to secure. Turn under the ends of the tape, then machine-sew a second row of stitches 1.25cm (½in) from the first over the folds and through the tape. The folded pleats will form a zigzag hem along the diagonal bottom edge. Repeat to make the other tail. Align the pleated edge of each tail to the outer edge of the corresponding swag; staple the tails to the board. Fold the tape and fabric into mitered corners around the corner of the board and wrap the ends around the returns then staple.

11 Staple the corded tassels to the centre of the board staggering them at different levels. Stretch the flanged rope around the top perimeter edge of the swags and staple in place.

12 Attach L-shaped brackets to the underside of the board. Hold the board over the window and mark the positions of the screw holes for the pelmet brackets, as well as for the curtain rail. Drill starter holes into the wall. Mount the curtain rail, using appropriate fixings, and then hook up the curtains (see pages 40–3 for how to make basic flat panel curtains). Finally, screw the L-shaped brackets into place to secure the board holding the swags and tails.

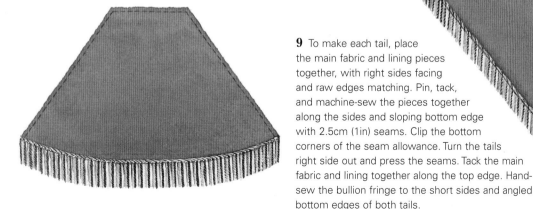

Fabric-covered Lambrequin

Covered with a pretty printed fabric, this fixed lambrequin with its matching lined Roman blind, adds character and charm to a wide recessed bathroom window in a country house. Its scrolled edge can be easily cut with a table saw and jigsaw attachment, but can also be accomplished with a bit more effort by hand using a coping saw or jigsaw. A layer of wadding (batting) between the board and the fabric gives the lambrequin a subtle softness, and highlighting the curves, a slim line of piping covered with matching fabric provides a crisp finishing touch.

MATERIALS

- Main fabric, including enough for piping (for measuring tips, see pages 179–81)
- Plain backing fabric
- Cotton wadding (batting)
- Piping cord
- Staple gun and staples
- Fabric adhesive or fusible webbing
- Sewing kit (see pages 170–3)

To make the lambrequin frame, you will need:
- Medium-density fibreboard (MDF), 0.75–1.25cm (¼–½) thick
- L-shaped brackets and appropriate screws
- Tools and fixings for cutting the board and attaching the lambrequin to the wall, including sandpaper and a tack cloth

This fabric-covered lambrequin frames the view from a window. The matching lined Roman blind provides privacy and warmth.

1 Measure the inside width of the window frame to get the finished width of the lambrequin. Measure the inside height of the window frame and divide by three to get the finished height of the lambrequin. Mark a rectangle equal to these dimensions on pattern paper. Cut out the shape and fold it in half crosswise. Draw half the scrolled lines and arch shape on the folded paper with the peak of the arch at the centre fold line. Cut out the shape and open out the paper.

2 Tape the pattern to the MDF and trace the shape. Using a table saw, or a coping saw or jigsaw, cut out the shape from the board. Use sandpaper to smooth off the rough edges. Remove the dust with a tack cloth.

3 Place the main fabric face down on a work surface with the grain vertical and the pattern square. Place the shaped MDF board on top of the fabric, centring it over the pattern repeat. Trace around the shape with a pencil or marker pen.

4 Cut out the main fabric, 1.25cm (½in) larger than the marked pencil or pen lines all around.

5 Cut a piece of wadding 5cm (2in) larger than the face of the shaped board all around. Stretch it over the face of the board and around to the back. Staple it in place; start at the top, then do the bottom; snip into the wadding to allow a smooth wrap around the curves. Finish by stapling the sides.

6 Measure, mark, and cut a strip of main fabric 10cm (4in) wide and equal in length to the perimeter of the scrolled board plus 5cm (2in). Set this strip aside.

7 Using the main fabric, make enough covered piping (see pages 176–7) to run around the entire perimeter of the scrolled board plus 5cm (2in).

8 Place the cut, shaped fabric panel right side up on a work surface and, with right sides facing and raw edges matching, pin and tack the piping and the long 10cm (4in) wide strip of fabric to the fabric cover all around, starting at one upper corner and sandwiching the piping between the layers. Using a piping foot (see page 178), machine-stitch the layers together with 1.25cm (½in) seams, folding in and trimming the edges of the piping and fabric strip. Turn right side out and press.

9 Place the cover face up over the padded board. Stretch the strip around to the back and staple in place making sure the piping lies straight and flush with the board edges all around.

10 Use the paper template to trace the lambrequin shape onto the plain backing fabric. Fold in and press 2.5cm (1in) all around the perimeter of the backing fabric, clipping or folding under at the corners to keep the folded edges smooth. Use fabric adhesive or fusible webbing to affix the backing over the stapled edge of the fabric on the back of the lambrequin.

11 Screw 2 or 3 L-shaped brackets to the top of the lambrequin. Hold it up to the window recess and mark the positions of the screw holes through the brackets. Using appropriate fixings and tools, attach the lambrequin to the wall.

Fabric-covered Lambrequin　79

Zigzag Pelmet

Made of a lively red-and-white ticking stripe, floor-length curtains topped with a zigzag-edged pelmet add playful punch to a large bay window in this casual family room. The wide contrasting border and whimsical tassels call attention to the pelmet's serrated edge, which echoes the lines of the window. A more subtle but equally appealing variation of this pelmet could be made by forgoing the zigzag edge and tassels while preserving the contrasting band along a straight bottom edge. Attached to ceiling- or wall-mounted boards with hook-and-loop (touch-and-close) tape, the pelmet is easy to remove for cleaning.

MATERIALS

- Main fabric (for measuring tips, see pages 179–81)
- Contrasting fabric for edging
- Tassels
- Hook-and-loop (touch-and-close) tape, 2cm (¾in) wide
- Staple gun and staples
- Fusible webbing or an iron-on fabric stiffener
- Sewing kit (see pages 170–3)
- Triangle or set square (optional)

To make the pelmet frame, you will need:
- Medium-density fibreboard (MDF) or plywood, 2.5cm (1in) thick by 5–10cm (2–4in) wide
- L-shaped brackets and screws (optional)
- Tools and fixings for cutting the board and attaching the pelmet to the wall, including sandpaper, and mitre saw and mitre box (optional)

opposite A zigzag-edged pelmet finished with contrasting trim and tassels gives this room an air of exuberance. (The cover on the wingchair in the window is featured on pages 158–61.)

1 Measure the width and total height of the window treatment, including the space needed for the curtains to be drawn back, and the length of the curtains covered by the pelmet, as well as the depth of the returns to accommodate the brackets supporting the curtain rail (see pages 179–81). Use this to determine the cut width of the pelmet boards. If your window is flat, you'll need three pieces – one for the front of the window and two for the returns. If you have a bay window, as here, you'll need five pieces, one for the centre, two for each angled side, and two for the returns. (Note: The returns should be about 5–12.5cm/3–5in deep, depending on the space required by the curtain rail and its brackets.) Measure, mark, and cut the wood pieces, using a handsaw or table saw. If you have a bay window, use a mitre saw and mitre box to cut the ends of the board to fit flush.

2 If you are mounting the boards to the ceiling, attach L-shaped brackets to their undersides. If you are mounting the boards to the wall, you will need specialist brackets. Holding the boards in place, either at the desired height against the wall or flush with the ceiling, mark screw holes through the brackets and into the wall or through the boards into the ceiling at the ends of the boards; with long boards you will also need to fix the centres. Attach the boards to the wall or ceiling using appropriate tools and fixings.

3 To determine the cut width of the pelmet fabric, measure the entire width of the mounted boards and add 5cm (2in). To determine the cut height, divide the total window treatment height (from ceiling to floor if there will be floor-length curtains or from ceiling to the bottom of the window sill, if not) by 5 and add 2.5cm (1in). Measure, mark, and cut a piece of main fabric and fusible webbing or iron-on fabric stiffener to these dimensions. Iron the webbing or stiffener to the wrong side of the fabric and lay on a work surface.

4 To determine the finished width of the top of each zigzag, divide the width of the window by the number of zigzags that you require and make sure that both ends stop on a half or a whole zigzag. As a guide, each zigzag should be 15–25cm (6–10in). Using a set square and a ruler, calculate the zigzag outline accurately on the wrong side of the panel of main fabric and mark off the zigzags with a marker pen. Cut out the zigzags, leaving a 2.5cm (1in) straight edge perpendicular to each short end (plus the width of the board if your pelmet is over a bay window, as here, see diagram step 11). Fold under and press 1.25cm (½in) double hems along each short end and hand-sew with hemming stitch (see page 174).

5 Measure, mark, and cut strips of contrasting fabric to trim the edges of each zigzag, include short pieces for the ends of the pelmet board if applicable. Make them 6.25cm (2½in) wide and add 2.5cm (1in) to each length for turning under by 1.25cm (½in) at the ends.

continued over >>

>> continued

6 Place two strips right sides together, pinning and folding one of the ends of each strip on the diagonal to form a V-shape that fits the peak of the zigzag; press the folds. Machine-stitch the two strips together along the crease line, stopping short of the edges to turn the allowances. Snip away the excess of the mitred corner and repeat for all remaining strips that will form the trimmed edge, including the short end pieces.

7 Open out each V-shaped strip. Press open the seams, then fold under and press over all the raw edges by 1.25cm (½in) towards the wrong side of the fabric, including the short end strips.

8 If you're wrapping the ends of the fabric around the ends of the board, place a short end strip on the right side of the fabric, slightly extending below the lower raw edge, then position a V-shape over the first zigzag, folding under, pinning, and pressing the ends to form neat joins with the short strip on one side and the next V-shape on the other. Continue in this way, placing V-shapes to the other end, finishing with a short piece if necessary. Machine-topstitch both sides of the strips to the pelmet, using an edging foot (see page 178) if you have one. Or hand-sew the strips to the fabric if preferred.

opposite page Picking up on the fanciful skirt of a fitted loose sofa cover, deep, softly gathered pelmets with zig-zag hems dress up a pair of windows.

9 Hand-sew a tassel to the point of each zigzag. (These tassels have pre-attached rings, but any kind of tassle could be used.)

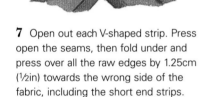

10 Fold over and press the top edge of the pelmet 1.25cm (½in) towards the wrong side of the fabric.

11 Cut a strip of hook-and-loop tape equal to the length of the pelmet. Separate the two sides of the strip and hand-sew or machine-stitch one side to the top of the back of the pelmet hiding the raw allowance. Press the pelmet.

12 Staple the other side of the tape along the pelmet board. Join the strips to mount the pelmet.

blinds

As a simpler, more streamlined approach to window dressing replaces the highly decorative curtains and elaborate swags of the past, the beauty of blinds has never held more appeal. Not only are they eminently practical – lined versions control glare, provide insulation, and conceal unwanted views, while sheer ones let in light and provide privacy – they're also stylistically versatile. Simple Roman blinds in plain-woven linen or crisp roller blinds made of light-as-air voile provide the perfect finishing touch to contemporary spaces. Trimmed with ribbon or rick rack and made from a gingham or calico cotton, these treatments would also add colour and charm to relaxed country settings. And blinds that have a slightly more complex construction, such as soft London blinds with inverted pleats, or billowy gathered Austrian blinds, can bring richness and character to traditional or polished rooms. Mounted outside the window frame, they can make small windows look grand and heighten the overall sense of space, while set inside the frame they add softness and show off elegant mouldings at the same time. Although blinds can refer to constructions of wood or metal, those described here, and featured in the projects (see pages 94–105), are fabric-based.

blind
INSPIRATION

As with curtains, choosing an appropriate style for your blinds will depend on the style and character of your windows and other architectural features of the room, as well as on the overall decorative qualities you aim to achieve. It will also depend on whether you plan to use your blinds alone or with any other treatments, such as curtains or pelmets. For example, if you are also using curtains, you may want the blinds simply as a sun screen, rather than for privacy as well.

left Inpired by a classic simplicity, this plain Roman blind, with its contrasting inset band, enhances the proportions of a tall window.
above Mounted beneath a sweeping swag and flowing curtains in a sheer white fabric, a bold roller blind provides interest and contrast.

Selecting a Style

Before settling on a style, ask yourself several relevant questions. Will the blind be primarily functional, serving to control light and add privacy? Or will it be decorative, adding layers of softness or contributing energy to a colour scheme? Do you want your blinds to solve design flaws, such as concealing a less-than-perfect view or enlarging the appearance of small windows? Will they be used alone? Or will they be layered with other treatments? Will they be inside-mounted, that is, affixed inside the window frame, or outside mounted, attached to a rod or mounting board and positioned outside and above the window frame? What is the overall decorative spirit of the room – formal or casual, contemporary or traditional? The answers to these questions will help you come up with a checklist that can guide your style and fabric selections to create a blind that properly addresses your needs and goals.

top left The graphic black-and-white stripes of these simple Roman blinds echo the smaller-scale stripes of the cushions on the sofa in a modern living room.
top right With their beaded trim and playful pattern, these large Roman blinds introduce lots of colour in a contemporary room.
left Suspended with skinny ties, sheer roll-up blinds provide a touch of softness and light-control in a sunny corner.

top left Venetian and striped balloon blinds are successfully paired in this formal foyer.
centre A vivid red-and-yellow *toile de Jouy* ensures this blind makes a strong statement.
top right Behind sheer muslin curtains, a red-and-white Roman blind adds colour in a bedroom.
above Inverted pleats on this blind provide a romantic touch.

Types of Blinds

Gaining a clear idea of the varieties of blinds available will help you choose a style that works for you. In general there are four types of blinds – Austrian, balloon, roller, and Roman.

Austrian blinds are made using soft fabrics and feature tightly shirred, draping scallops running their entire length. They are drawn up from the bottom by means of cords and rings, and create horizontal folds when raised. They are often shirred along their width as well as the length by means of shirring tape. They take a lot of fabric, requiring up to three times the height of the window and are sometimes referred to as festoon blinds.

Balloon blinds are also soft fabric with deep inverted pleats that fall into airy, rounded folds at the bottom. Their puffy appearance requires extra fabric across the width. Specialized tapes can be used to create the gathered balloon shapes. London blinds with inverted pleats, opera blinds and cloud blinds, which are gathered across the top as well as from the hem, fall into this category.

Roller blinds are flat fabric blinds attached to a roller mechanism, usually by means of a slat inserted into a groove in the roller or with adhesive. They provide the sleekest profile, but their hems are often shaped, scalloped, or otherwise trimmed for decorative flourish.

Roman blinds are drawn up from the bottom by means of cords and rings and create neat horizontal folds when raised. When down, a standard Roman blind panel is flat. Hobbled Roman blinds have built-in folds that remain in place when the blind is down (see pages 102–5). Dowelled, slouched, and stagecoach blinds are other variations on the Roman blind.

Fabrics and Linings

The answers to your aesthetic and functional questions will enable you to choose an appropriate fabric. For simple blinds designed to add privacy and soften light, a wide range of sheer fabrics can be used to create anything from crisp roller blinds to densely shirred Austrian blinds, or simple Roman blinds (see pages 94–7). When using blinds alone or

top left Edged with wide contrasting black bands, a plain natural linen Roman blind brings a modern practical air to this country bathroom.

above The red-and-white *toile de Jouy* used for this simple Roman blind harmonizes with the similarly coloured fabrics on other soft furnishings in a cosy and restful window area.

far left Slim contrasting taupe bands give a subtle definition to this creamy Roman blind in a contemporary bedroom.

left In this drawing room, a Roman blind in a strong black-and-white print matches the fabric covering the walls. A red bow at the top of the blind provides a vivid finishing touch.

Blind Inspiration   89

opposite Sheer Roman blinds
with integrated dowels give the
windows of a contemporary
room a crisp, streamlined finish.
top left This London blind is
made from a tea-dyed printed
linen, which gives the bedroom
a look of faded elegance.
centre Although mounted on a
basic roller mechanism, the lace
fabric and light fringe on this
blind ensure its romantic appeal.
top right It is the wrought-iron
pole with heart-shaped finials
that give this Roman blind its
charm. The fabric is edged with
bias-cut self-piping.

layered with over-treatments as additional
decorative elements, light- to medium-weight
woven fabrics and prints can enliven a room
with colour and pattern (see pages 98–101). If
you choose a patterned fabric, remember that
the size and scale of the pattern repeat should
complement the size and scale of the window
and the dominant design should be centred.
If your windows are wide, you'll need to join
widths and match patterns along either side
of a central width (see pages 165–6).

If you aim to control or completely black-out
light with your blinds, or if you want them to
provide a layer or insulation, you'll need to
line them with a suitable material. Lining your
blind will also enable you to protect the face
fabric from dust, deterioration, and fading.
Bear in mind that linings add weight and
thickness. Choosing light- or medium-weight
fabrics will usually result in the most graceful
folds or shirring.

Mounts and Pulls

Whether your blind will be inside- or outside-
mounted will depend on the material and
depth of your window frame, the type of wall,
and the space above and around the frame.
Never opt for an inside-mounted blind if your
window frames are made of metal or vinyl.
If the blind is to be used with other over
treatments, the brackets of the rail for any
curtains as well as the depth of the mounting
board for a pelmet will need to clear any
projection of an outside-mounted blind board
or rod. As with curtains and top treatments, it
is vital to choose appropriate wall anchors to
ensure the blind is fixed securely.

Since blinds are operated by a looped cord
or series of cords, it is important to determine
the side on which the cords will hang for easy
operation before the blind is fabricated and
installed. The cords will need to wrap around a
cleat mounted to the wall in order for the blind

to remain raised when required. The cleat and the blind pull afford additional decorative opportunities, so choose styles or materials that harmonize with other decorative elements in the room. And while most blinds are drawn open from the bottom up, you can also consider mechanisms that allow them to be operated from the top down.

Finishing Touches

Just like curtains, blinds are often embellished with decorative details to add personality and polish. If mounted on rods, their top edges can be gathered or shaped with scalloped or tab tops. The sides of a blind can be dressed up with contrasting borders, braids, or ribbon trims. Inverted pleats may be made with a contrasting fabric, and folds can be accented with buttons or rosettes. Hems can be highlighted with borders, ruffles, beads, bows, or pretty ties. They can also be shaped with scallops, zigzags, or any number of cutout designs and accented with decorative trims, such as gimps, fringes, and braids.

above and inset A trio of fabric panels serve as shutter blinds on tall, floor-to-ceiling windows. Suspended from portière rods on hinges, they can be swung open or closed to control sunlight and provide privacy.
top right Mounted on a sliding track, these sheer fabric panels give a contemporary room modern polish.
right Topped with thin muslin curtains, this cheerful red-and-white gingham blind calls attention to a charming circular window.

Decorative touches

1 Decorative ties
Long cotton ties fixed in a bow
hold a cotton seersucker blind at
the desired height. Cotton ties
are quick and easy to make and
would look equally good in a
contrasting fabric.

SEE **PAGE 46, STEPS 2–4, FOR MAKING TIES**

2 Ruffled edge
A frilled edge gives a flirty finish
to a simple Roman blind made
of matelassé in a pale lilac hue.
Ruffles, which are made from a
length of fabric hemmed along
one edge and gathered along
the other, are a straightforward
personal touch that could be
added to almost any blind.

3 Lace trim
A pretty crocheted lace border
with a zigzag edge adds a
decorative flourish to a simple
Holland blind. New and vintage
crocheted lace borders can be
readily found at textile shops
and on-line sites and are easy
to attach to the hems of basic
blinds by machine or by hand.

4 Contrast edging
A linen roll-up blind with a
checked border is trimmed with
matching ties, which enable its
height to be adjusted. Similar
borders and ties can be simply
applied with grosgrain and other
ribbon trims.

SEE **CRISP ROMAN BLIND, PAGES 94–7**

Crisp Roman Blind

Few window treatments are as popular or versatile as classic Roman blinds. Their crisp lines and tailored pleats make them ideal for streamlined interiors or extra large windows that open onto beautiful views, yet they work equally well on small windows in traditional rooms. When made from a solid or subtle tone-on-tone woven damask, they seem to meld with the architecture. But, in a bold stripe or lively print fabric, they can also introduce a shot of colour or pattern to a room.

MATERIALS

- Main fabric (for measuring tips, see pages 179–81)
- Accent fabric
- Lining fabric
- Tack-on rings and/or blind rings
- Tacking tool (optional)
- Cord
- Staple gun and staples
- Sewing kit (see pages 170–3)
- Screw eyes
- Cleat and cord pull
- Steel rod or wooden dowel, 6mm (¼in) diameter
- Mounting board, 2.5cm (1in) by 5cm (2in)
- Tools and fixings for cutting the board and attaching the blind to the wall

Making soft folds of neutral fabric, enlivened with a contrasting edge, these Roman blinds quietly dress the windows without blocking the view.

1 Measure the height and width of the window frame. (Note: The blinds on these windows were mounted directly to the ceiling in front of the metal frames, and so were measured from the outside height and width of the frames. For traditional wood framed, measure from inside the frame and mount to the top of the frame.) Cut a mounting board 1.25cm (½in) shorter than the width of the frame, using a handsaw. Cut the steel rod or wooden dowel to the same length with a hacksaw.

2 Measure and mark the positions of the screws along the centre of one side of the mounting board, about 5cm (2in) from either end and evenly spaced about 30cm (12in) apart between the outer holes. Position the board into place on the ceiling or the top of the frame and drill screw holes through the board and into the window frame or ceiling.

3 To get the cut dimensions of the blind, add 15cm (6in) to the height and 5cm (2in) to the width. Cut a piece of main fabric to these dimensions, making sure the grain is straight and the edges are square. You may need to join widths to get the desired width. If so, calculate the number of widths you'll need and join widths or portions of widths, matching patterns as necessary, to get the desired size, making sure to join portions of widths on either side of a full central width of fabric (see pages 165–6).

4 Repeat for the lining, making the cut length the same as for the main fabric and the width equal to the width of the mounting board.

5 On a work surface, centre the lining over the main fabric, right sides facing and top and bottom raw edges matching. The main fabric will extend 2.5cm (1in) on either side of the lining. Pin the side edges together; machine-sew with 1.25cm (½in) seams. Press the seams towards the inside of the blind. Turn right side out.

continued over >>

6 Tack the lining to the main fabric along the bottom 1.25cm (½in) from the raw edge. Finish the top edge, joining the main fabric to the lining using overcast stitch and an edging foot (see page 178).

7 Fold under and press the bottom raw edge 1.25cm (½in) towards the wrong side of the blind. Fold under and press the bottom hem another 10cm (4in) toward the wrong side. Unfold the hem.

8 Measure, mark, and cut a strip of accent fabric equal to the cut width of the mounting board plus 2.5cm (1in), by 6.25cm (2½in) wide.

9 Place the accent band, wrong side up, on top of the blind. Position then pin, one long raw edge 2.5cm (1in) from the inside folded edge (step 7) and the raw short edges extending from the sides of the blind by 1.25cm (½in). Machine-stitch the band to the blind; use an edge/quilting guide (see page 178) along the fold line to keep the band straight.

10 Fold and press the band over the stitch line so the right side faces up. Measure, fold under, and press the raw edge so its folded edge is flush with the inner fold line of the blind; fold in and press the short ends flush with sides of the blind. Machine-topstitch the sides and bottom of the band to the blind. Fold up the hem of the blind and machine-topstitch to close.

11 Press the blind. Place it, face down, on a work surface. Measure and mark the position of the tack-on rings. Start the first two rings of the bottom row along the top of the hem, 1.25cm (½in) from each side edge. Mark the position of the remaining rings in the bottom row, spacing them about 25cm (10in) apart.

12 Measure and mark the positions of the remaining rings, evenly spacing them about every 20cm (8in) above each ring in the first row along the hem, stopping about 20–25cm (8–10in) from the top edge. Using the tacking tool, insert rings into every mark on the back of the blind. Or, hand-sew the rings to the back of the blind if you prefer. Cut one length of cord for each column of rings equal to twice the length plus the width of the blind. Tie a length of cord to each of the bottom rings along the hem and thread them through the subsequent rings in each column.

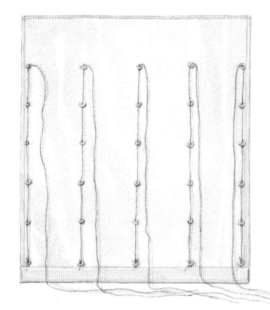

13 Fold over and press the top edge of the blind 5cm (2in) towards the lining side. Align the folded edge with the front of the mounting board, centring the blind on the board. Attach the blind to the top of the board using the staple gun. Place the blind wrong side up on a work surface and stretch the cords up to the underside of the mounting board and mark the positions of the screw eyes in alignment with the cords. Drill starter holes for the screw eyes with a very narrow bit if necessary and insert the screw eyes into the mounting board.

14 Determine from which side you want the cord to hang, then string the cords through the screw eye above each column of rings and across the top though the other screw eyes towards the side from which the cord will hang.

15 Mount the blind into the starter holes. Insert the steel rod into the pocket of the hem. Allow the blind to hang fully open and draw the cords even on one side, trimming the excess and knotting them together in several places. Attach the pull. Screw a cleat into the wall or window frame and raise the blind to the desired height, smoothing the folds.

Arch-topped Roman Blind

Windows topped with arches can give wonderful architectural interest to a room, but they can also be a problem to dress. Elaborate upholstered cornices or shaped canopies with projecting bowed ribs are suitable for sophisticated spaces. But relaxed rooms in country settings call for a simpler approach. Fortunately, it is relatively easy to cut a mounting board to fit an arched shape and cover it simply with a cheery casual fabric that extends into a pleated Roman blind. As with a basic Roman blind, the perimeter can be highlighted with contrasting ribbon or trim or, for additional flourish, the bottom edge could be scalloped to echo the shape of the arch at the top.

MATERIALS

- Main fabric (for measuring tips, see pages 179–81)
- Lining fabric
- Tack-on rings and/or blind rings
- Cord
- Staple gun and staples
- Masking tapes
- Sewing kit (see page 170–3)
- Screw eyes
- Cleat
- Cord pull
- Stainless-steel rods, or plastic or wooden dowels, 6mm (¼in) diameter
- Medium-density fibreboard (MDF), 0.75–1.25cm (¼–½in) thick
- L-shaped brackets
- Tools and fixings for cutting the board and attaching the blind to the wall, including sandpaper and tack cloth

opposite A simple Roman blind with an arched top adds charm to a window seat in a country kitchen. Horizontal ribs have been made with dowels inserted into pockets sewn into the lining to keep the pleats crisp across the wide expanse.

1 Cut a piece of pattern paper longer than the width of the window and tape it over the window arch. Trace along the curved line of the arch. Remove the paper and cut out the shape. Tape the pattern to the MDF and trace the shape onto the board. Cut out the curved outline with a coping saw or jigsaw. Sand the edges of the board to smooth. Wipe off the dust with a tack cloth.

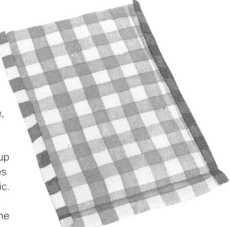

2 Measure the width and vertical drop of the window from the top of the arch to the sill. Add 17.5cm (7in) to the width measurement and 22.5cm (9in) to the length measurement. Measure, mark, and cut a piece of main fabric to these dimensions, making sure the grain is straight and the pattern is square. Place the fabric wrong side up on a work surface. Fold in and press the side edges 8.75cm (3½in) towards the wrong side of the fabric. Fold in and press the bottom edge by 17.5cm (7in), then open out the fold. The folded edge denotes the bottom edge of the finished blind.

3 Measure, mark, and cut a piece of lining fabric 12.5cm (5in) wider and 22.5cm (9in) longer than width and maximum vertical drop dimensions of the window. Add an additional 2.5cm (1in) of length for every dowel that will be in the blind. Cut out the lining fabric. Place the lining wrong side up on a work surface and fold in and press the side edges by 7.5 cm (3in) towards the wrong side of the fabric. Turn the lining over flat.

4 Cut the dowels 1.25cm (½in) shorter than the finished width of the blind. To calculate the positions of the dowel pockets on the lining, divide the drop of the window from the bottom of the arch to the sill by the number of desired pockets. (The first pocket should be 7.5cm/3in from the bottom edge of the lining and the last pocket should be about 7.5cm/3in below the bottom of the arch; the others should be positioned about 20cm/8in apart.) Using a ruler and T-square, mark the positions of the pockets across the lining.

5 Measure the circumference of a dowel. Fold in, mark, and pin folds, so that each side of the fold equals 1.25cm (½in) at each mark across the lining, adding an extra pinch to accommodate the dowels easily. Stitch across the lining at each mark to form the pockets.

6 Place the main fabric wrong side up on a work surface. Fold the bottom folded edge in half to create a 8.75cm (3½in) double hem.

7 Place the lining, right side up, over the main fabric. Slip the bottom raw edge of the lining under the folded hem of the main fabric, aligning the first pocket with the top folded edge of the hem and centring the lining so that the side edges are about 1.25cm (½in) narrower than the main fabric on each side. Pin the panels together all around.

8 Machine-stitch the lining to the main fabric, topstitching along the bottom of each pocket to join the layers together. Hand-sew the hem of the blind with hemming stitch (see page 174).

9 Insert a wooden dowel or rod into each pocket, and hand-sew to close the ends.

continued over >>

10 Mark the positions of each vertical column of rings along the bottom rod pocket (depending on the width of the window, there should be 3–8 columns, evenly spaced apart). Mark the positions of subsequent rings in each column on each pocket, directly above the starting rings along the hem. Hand-sew the rings to each mark. For each column of rings, cut a length of cord that is equal to twice the height plus the width of the blind. Knot each length of cord to a bottom ring, then thread it through the vertical column of rings above.

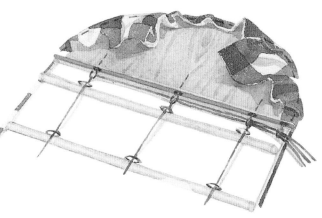

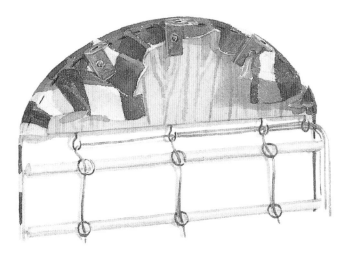

11 Place the curved MDF board across the top of the blind, centring it between the side edges with surplus fabric extending over the top edge. Wrap the excess fabric around to the back of the board, stretching and stapling the fabric to the board and creating a smooth surface on the front. Clip into the allowance at the bottom edge of the board if necessary to get a smooth fit.

12 Insert screw eyes into the base of the board just above each row of rings and at the side edge from which you want the cords to hang. Use a drill with a very narrow bit to create starter holes for the screw eyes if necessary. Draw the cords through the screw eyes directly above each column of rings, then draw the cords through the screw eyes across the blind towards the side on which the cords will hang.

13 Attach L-shaped brackets to the top of the board. Hold the board up to the arch and mark the positions of the screw holes. Mount the blind using appropriate fixings.

14 Allow the blind to hang to its maximum length. Even out the cords, knot them together at several points, cut off the excess to even off the ends, then thread the ends through the cord pull and knot off. Attach a cleat to the wall, pull up the cord to raise the blind, and wrap the cord around the cleat.

opposite page An attractive arched window has been enhanced with a sheer fabric Roman blind, gathered and shaped at the top to emphasize the curves.

Lined Hobbled Roman Blind

For anyone who likes the simplicity of a Roman blind but favours more softness, this hobbled Roman blind is the perfect choice. It is tailored like a basic Roman blind, but is made with twice or three times as much fabric. This is folded up creating built-in soft layers that provide fullness, even when the blind is down. The folds are produced with horizontal stays or ribs secured with twill tape. Hobbled Roman blinds are typically executed in a two-to-one ratio, like those shown here, or a three-to-one ratio. A two-to-one ratio produces a striped effect as light passes through one layer of fabric between the folds and three layers along them, while a three-to-one ratio controls light evenly since three layers of fabric overlap the entire length of the blind.

MATERIALS

- Main fabric (for measuring tips, see pages 179–81)
- Lining fabric
- Twill tape
- Tack-on rings and/or blind rings
- Cord
- Staple gun and staples
- Sewing kit (see pages 170–3)
- Screw eyes
- Cleat and cord pull
- Plastic or wooden dowels, 6mm (¼in) diameter
- Mounting board, 2.5cm (1in) by 10cm (4in)
- L-shaped brackets
- Tools and fixings for cutting the board and attaching the blind to the wall

opposite Built-in folds of fabric in these hobbled Roman blinds lend subtle textural interest to a contemporary neutral room.

1 Measure the desired finished height and width of the blind. (Note: The blinds on these glazed doors were mounted just below the cornice and so their length was measured from the top of the intended position of the mounting board to the floor, and their width was measured between the outsides of the door frames. For traditional wood window frames, you could also measure inside the frame and mount the blind to the top of the frame, see pages 180–1.) Cut a mounting board to the desired finished width. Cut several plastic or wooden dowels 1.25cm (½in) shorter than the desired finished width of the blind with a hacksaw.

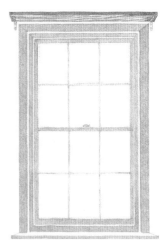

2 To determine the cut dimensions of the blind, add 5cm (2in) to the desired finished width; double (or triple) the desired finished height and add 22.5cm (9in). Cut a piece of main fabric to these dimensions with the grain straight and the edges square. If you need to join fabric widths to get the required blind width, calculate the number of widths you'll need and join widths or portions of widths, matching patterns as necessary (see pages 179–81).

3 Repeat for the lining, making the cut length the same as for the main fabric and the cut width equal to the width of the mounting board.

4 On a work surface, centre the lining over the main fabric, right sides facing, top and bottom raw edges matching. The main fabric will extend 2.5cm (1in) on each side of the lining fabric. Pin the side edges together; machine-stitch with 1.25cm (½in) seams. Press the seams towards the inside of the blind. Turn right side out.

5 Tack the lining to the main fabric along the bottom, 1.25cm (½in) from the raw edge. Finish the top edge, joining the main fabric to the lining with overcast stitch and using an edging foot (see page 178).

continued over >>

6 Fold under and press the bottom raw edge by 1.25cm (½in) towards the wrong side. Fold under and press the bottom hem another 5cm (2in) towards the wrong side. Machine-topstitch close to the fold to close the hem.

7 Place the blind, face down on a work surface. Measure and mark the position of the dowel pockets. The first pocket starts 20cm (8in) above the bottom of the finished hem. Each subsequent pocket will be 27.5cm (11in) from the preceding pocket, with the last one located about 20cm (8in) from the top edge. Fold and press a crease along the width of each marked pocket position. Sew across the blind 1.25cm (½in) from each crease to create the pockets.

8 Cut 3 or 4 lengths of twill tape, 10cm (4in) shorter than the finished length of the blind. Using a pencil or fabric marker, make a mark every 13.25cm (5¼in) on each strip of twill tape. Place a strip of tape down the length of the blind, about 5–7.5cm (2–3in) from one side. Pleat the fabric above and below each mark so that the marks on the twill tape align with the edges of the dowel pockets. Hand-sew the rings through the twill tape and catch a small amount of the pocket edge (or machine zigzag-stitch with the feed dogs down). Repeat on the other side of the blind, and then for all other strips of twill tape and rings, evenly spacing them in the centre of the blind.

9 Cut one length of cord for each vertical column of rings, equal to twice the length plus the width of the blind. Tie the cords to the bottom rings of each column along the hem and thread them up through the subsequent rings in each column.

10 Cut two pieces of main fabric and two pieces of lining fabric all measuring 11.25 by 15cm (4½ by 6in). Place the lining fabric pieces over the main fabric pieces, with right sides facing and raw edges matching. Sew around the sides and one short end with 1.25cm (½in) seams. Clip the corners, turn right side out. Fold in and press the raw edges by 1.25cm (½in); machine-topstitch to close. Fold and press the topstitched short side of each piece 2.5cm (1in) towards the wrong side. Open out the fold, align the crease with the short ends of the mounting board and staple the 2.5cm (1in) flaps to the top of the board.

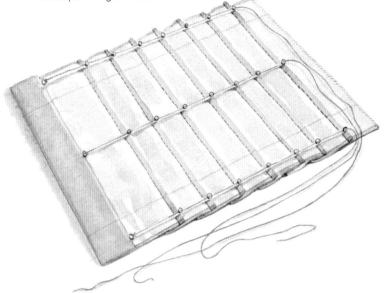

11 Fold over and press the top edge of the blind 9cm (3½in) towards the lining side. Align the folded edge with the front of the mounting board, centring the blind. Attach the blind to the top of the board using the staple gun.

12 Place the blind and board wrong side up on a work surface and stretch the cords up to the underside of the mounting board. Mark the positions of the screw eyes in alignment with the cords. Drill starter holes for the screw eyes with a very narrow bit if necessary and insert the screw eyes into the mounting board.

13 Determine from which side you want the cord to hang and string the cords through the screw eye above each vertical column of rings, across the top and though the other screw eyes towards the side from which the cord will hang.

14 Attach the L-shaped brackets to the underside of the board. Hold the board up to the wall and mark the positions of the screw holes. Mount the blind using appropriate fixings.

15 Insert the plastic or wooden dowels into the pockets and hand-sew the openings closed if desired. Allow the blind to hang fully open and draw the cords evenly on one side, trimming the excess and knotting them together at several points. Attach the cord pull. Screw the cleat into the wall or window frame and raise the blind to the desired height, wrap the cord around the cleat, and smooth the folds of the blind.

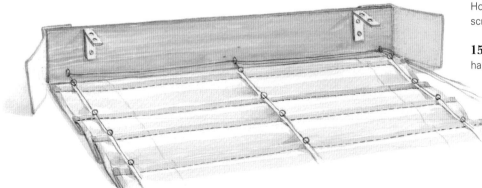

cushions

Cushions are to the home what comfort food is to the body – ultimate feel-good essentials that sustain the spirit and soften the hard knocks of daily life. But, like a great handbag or fabulous pair of shoes, they can also elevate an ordinary ensemble by providing a touch of luxury. Whether a simple scatter cushion, a custom-crafted chair pad, or a decorative bolster, a cushion is typically a small, portable accent piece, making it easy to swap for a seasonal change of scene (the projects on pages 116–25 provide plenty of ideas). A cushion's compact size also gives you a licence to splurge on costly fabrics or trims that can add pops of colour or unexpected texture to a room. And, as small-scale accoutrements, cushions are ideal for experimenting with pattern, offering a means for taking chances and shaking up a space with shots of personality or adding energy with visual grace notes or elements of surprise. Since cushions are meant to come in contact with the skin, chose fabrics for their tactile qualities – appealing to the touch as much as to the eye.

cushions

FOR EVERY OCCASION

Whether you use them casually to feather your nest or lavishly to inject a note of glamour, cushions are little things that can add a lot of comfort – and style – to a room. Covered with a pretty floral print and edged with a wide, floppy ruffle, a small accent cushion can introduce a dollop of charm in a feminine room. Wrapped in an extravagant silk-velvet and edged with thick welting, a pair of down-filled bolsters can enrich an antique daybed with a luxurious finishing touch. Or topped with a vibrant, durable outdoor fabric, tufted chair pads can add zing to an alfresco table setting. Selecting a fabric that's suitable for its intended purpose will ensure that the cushion harmonizes with its surroundings and enhances the overall ambience. Providing a cushion with an appropriate filler is essential to its comfort and longevity.

left A mass of cushions in various shapes and sizes and covered with a mix of fabrics in different colours transforms a bed into a sofa.
above A collection of white cushions with lace-and-crochet flanges adds a romantic touch to a contemporary sofa covered in white linen.

far left Quilted cushions in checks and stripes lend relaxed comfort to an outdoor bent-willow bench.
left Trimmed with bands cut on the bias and adorned with bows, simple checked cushions are given extra polish.
below Vintage textiles add punch to the seat cushion and bolster on an antique daybed.

Types of Cushion

Decorative cushions come in all shapes and sizes, and serve a variety of purposes in different rooms. Scatter cushions, for example, provide an extra touch of soft support to upholstered chairs and sofas. Typically square or rectangular, they usually range in size from 25–75cm (10–30in) and can be covered to match the fabric of an upholstered piece or topped with a contrasting fabric to add colour and texture to a room. Accent cushions, on the other hand, come in all shapes and sizes; they are often covered with highly decorative fabrics or embellished with embroidery and trims, and are specifically designed to add a decorative dimension to beds and upholstered seating.

Thick, large-scale floor cushions are usually made with removable covers and even equipped with handles for easy transport. Even thicker and more durable are pouffes or hassocks. They are often cylindrical or cube-shaped and offer a firmer form of seating or footrest. Sometimes reinforced with internal structural supports, they are frequently filled with paper, horsehair, or foam

above These cushions in woven cream jacquard, edged with fancy cord, provide softness on a couch covered in the same fabric and subtle contrast to the striped silk wallcovering.
top right Covered with a masculine stripe, these cushions on a cane chair are given a strong sense of identity.
right Simplicity is the key in this neat pairing of a checked cushion and black-piped chair seat. The geometric wall-covering emphasizes the point.

and covered with leather, which may be tooled or dyed. Beanbags, which function as extra-large floor cushions, are loosely filled and have malleable forms; they are usually covered in tough, brightly coloured fabrics.

Bolsters and neck rolls are available preformed in standard dimensions or can be custom-made to any size. They are basically cylindrical cushions used as arm props on sofas or as decorative head and neck rests on beds (see pages 116–17). Larger mattress-like cushions, traditionally called squabs, teamed with bolsters can be used on daybeds for a classy effect (see pages 124–5).

Chair pads, seat cushions, and boxed cushions can range in thickness from 2.5–7.5cm (1–3in) and may be preformed, stuffed with wadding, or cut to fit any size. They add comfort to hard dining and outdoor chairs, as well as window seats and benches (see pages 122–3). Other decorative cushions can be shaped into novelty forms such as hearts or animal shapes to add a playful touch to children's rooms, crafted into bumpers to line baby cots, or cut to fit a pet's bed.

Casings and Covers

Most cushion forms are covered with a casing that holds the fibres, padding, or feathers that serve as the filler. These casings are usually made of a fine, tightly woven material, such as sateen or ticking, that keeps the filling in and dust out. In general, the casings are not removable; they should be hand-washed or dry cleaned, if necessary, with the filler still inside.

When it comes to covering a cushion, keeping in mind its primary purpose and the space in which it will be used will help you narrow down your fabric choices. For decorative cushions that will be used in living rooms or bedrooms, virtually anything goes – from embroidered cottons or luxurious silks to plush velvets, complex jacquards, or rich tapestries. Because cushions are relatively compact and usually require simple seams, heavier-weight fabrics, such as chenille or corduroy, can be fairly easily made into covers, too. Even lightweight fabrics, such as taffeta, can be suitable for decorative cushions. Their small size also allows cushions to be covered with remnants or scraps, which can be recycled and sewn into patchwork patterns, or

top left Chunky cotton fringes and insets made of vintage textiles give a pair of cushion covers a personal touch.
top centre This wicker chair cushion gets a note of polish with a short flange, cut on the bias and tucked at the corners.
above Embroidered with images of starfish and seashells, cotton pillows enrich a seaside bed.
far left This silk cushion with its appliqué birds introduces a note of modernity on a chaise longue.
left Gold braid and fabric remnants have been used to create coats of arms for the fronts of basic cushion covers.

even with woven pieces of leather, ribbon, or twill tape (see pages 118–21).

With the heavier use that floor cushions, chair pads, and outdoor cushions undergo, durable fabrics are best. Consider microsuede, twill, and canvas for indoor settings and fade-resistant acrylic twill or cotton canvas for outdoor environments. The same holds true for family rooms, where corduroy and chenille are other good options. These kinds of fabrics are also great for window seats and bench cushions.

below A small oblong silk cushion creates a sharp and graphic focal point on an elegant French settee.

Fillers and Foams

Things have come a long way since the earliest pillows, when straw was commonly used as a filler. Today, cushion inserts are made with everything from polyester to feathers, or even environmentally friendly bamboo fibres.

Polyester fibrefill consists of continuous filament synthetic fibres. It is the cheapest option and provides a good initial shape but loses its softness fairly quickly and becomes heavy and matted. A better grade of polyester is hollow-fill. This consists of continuous filament fibres with hollow cores and provides more softness for a longer period of time.

The most expensive filling is down, which is the light undercoating of waterfowl. Down consists of soft and fluffy, three-dimensional clusters of filaments growing from a central quill point, while feathers are flat and two-dimensional with a hard, tubular quill shaft. Feathers are strong, but not terribly soft. Many manufacturers combine both down and feather in order to make affordable, comfortable cushion and pillow fillers. Down and feather-and-down fillers are soft but they do need to be fluffed up regularly to preserve their shape. Hypoallergenic varieties are available.

Bamboo or cotton fibrefills are other natural cushion stuffings. Cotton can bunch over time, but bamboo fibres are strong with a high-lustre and a uniquely soft, silky texture that won't bunch or clump. Luxurious bamboo wadding gives quilts and clothing breathability, keeping you warm in colder climates and comfortably cool in warm climates.

For those who have allergies or suffer from other sensitivities or who prefer to use organic alternatives, buckwheat hulls are an option. Another choice is kapok, a golden silky fibre harvested from the seedpods of kapok trees. This sustainable rainforest crop is an almost magical material. Not only is it soft, smooth, hygienic, non-toxic, hypoallergenic, and environmentally friendly, it is also breathable and can be reused for generations without

developing mould or decaying. It even floats! An ancient treasure, it has long been used by Asian gurus and spiritual masters who have always appreciated its unique characteristics, such as its ability to conform to the body yet rebound instantly to its original fluffy shape.

It is possible to fill decorative cushions with scented herbs, such as rosemary and lavender. For beanbag cushions, expanded polystyrene beads are commonly used.

There are various foams that come in rolls or pre-cut forms, or can be cut and shaped to size. Foam is generally made of polyurethane, polyester, or latex. Polyurethane, a synthetic material, is flammable and some forms are liable to yellow, mildew, and crumble. Polyester, a flame-retardant synthetic, resists mildew, doesn't disintegrate or yellow and is non-allergenic. Latex, which is made from natural rubber, is resilient as well anti-microbial and hypoallergenic, but it is also flammable.

Embellishments and Edgings

Aside from the vast range of fabrics that can be creatively cut, combined, pleated, and tucked as covers for cushions, any number of interesting trims and embellishments may be used to further enhance and adorn them. Piping or welting – whether super thin or big and thick – provides a classic finish to the seams of all kinds of cushions, from a basic scatter cushion to an extravagant neck roll. But other options for edging cushions abound – narrow flange, wide ruffles, box-pleated trims, brush fringes, and crocheted edging to name but a few. Cushions can be personalized with embroidered monograms, embellished with beads, adorned with appliqué, banded with braids, or trimmed with tassels. Even their closures afford plenty of opportunities for creative expression. Buttons, bows, loops, tabs, and all kinds of ornamental trimmings can elevate these versatile decorative accents into finely crafted treasures.

top Edged with bold pendant borders, this pair of cushions gives a playful punch to a traditional sofa. The scalloped border of the checked oblong cushion helps to set them off.
above The romantic mood of a guest bedroom is enhanced by decorative pillows and a bolster covered with striped taffeta and trimmed with floral ruffles.

Decorative touches

1 Self-edges
Covered with cotton ticking and with folded Turkish corners, a casual cushion is trimmed with a band of matching fabric cut on the bias.

SEE PAGES **176–7** FOR MAKING BIAS BINDING

2 Appliqué
A simple white cotton cushion cover gets a lift with black wool appliqué. Attaching the shapes to the fabric with a fusible backing keeps them secure before machine- or hand-stitching in place.

SEE PAGES **120–1** FOR ADDING APPLIQUÉ

3 Lace border and ties
An antique cotton lace border adds charm to a checked cotton squab secured to a painted chair with long ties. The basic cushion is easy to make and fitting it to the chair with ties is also simple.

SEE PAGES **140–1** FOR CREATING SIMPLE CHAIR TIES

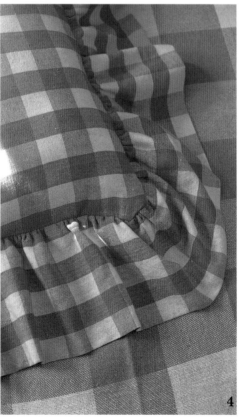

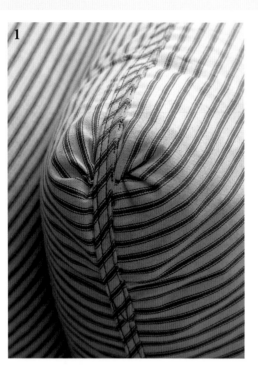

4 Ruffled flange
A wide gathered ruffle in a matching cotton fabric adds an air of softness and femininity to a pretty pillowcase. The small-scale check complements the larger-scaled pattern of the bedspread.

SEE PAGES **144–5** FOR ADDING RUFFLES

5 Tassels
This gorgeous cushion cover is made using a printed Fortuny fabric inset, bordered with linen and edged with a tassel fringe. Readymade tassel fringes come in a range of designs and give any cushion cover an elegant air.

6 Contrast piping

A Madras check pillow gets a sweet note of polish with slender piping covered in a skinny stripe.

SEE PAGES 176–7 FOR MAKING AND FITTING PIPING

7 Appliqué

Pale grey ultrasuede appliqué has been added on simple heavy white cotton pillowcases for an understated decorative finishing touch.

8 Tie closures

A simple striped cushion peeks out from the edge of an over-cover in a contrasting stripe edged with simple ties in matching fabric.

SEE PAGE 151, STEP 9, FOR MAKING FABRIC TIES

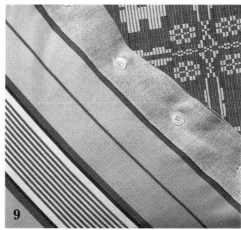

9–10 Button closures

Button plackets create a neat, easy-to-open closure for use in a variety of situations. Most sewing machines will sew buttonholes for you, but it is also satisfying to do them by hand.

SEE PAGES 174–5 FOR BUTTONHOLE STITCH

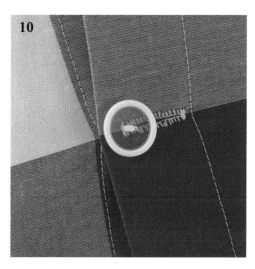

Simple Bolster Cover

Wrapped in a lovely tone-on-tone fabric with a subtle, intricate pattern, this long bolster serves as the pretty focal point of the bed. The cover was made without sewing as the hems and were created with fusible webbing and iron-on hook-and-loop tape. Wide satin ribbon bows secure the floppy gathered ends. If you can't find a long bolster, you can join two neck rolls and soften the join with wadding (batting), which requires some stitching. The bolster cover could also be sewn by topstitching the hook-and-loop tape and using hemming stitch for the hems.

MATERIALS

- Fabric
- Satin ribbon 2m (2yd)
- Bolster form: either one bolster 100cm (40in) long by 18cm (7in) in diameter, or two bolsters 50cm (20in) long by 12.5cm (5in) in diameter
- Fusible hook-and-loop (touch-and-close) tape
- Roll of fusible webbing, 3.75cm (1½in) wide
- Roll of fusible webbing, 6mm (¼in) wide
- Thin cotton wadding (batting)
- Sewing kit (see pages 170–3)

A simple-to-make cover in a serene pale blue jacquard fabric tied with a cream ribbon gives a bolster a pretty, polished appearance.

1 If you don't start with a bolster that is 100cm (40in) long, hand-sew two 50cm (20in) long bolster forms together to make one 100cm (40in) roll. If you sew two forms together and want to soften appearance and feel of the join between them, measure, mark, and cut a piece of thin cotton batting equal to twice the length of the bolster by its circumference.

Fold the wadding in half crosswise and wrap it around the bolster and hand-sew the seam along the length of the bolster.

2 Measure, mark, and cut a piece of fabric 190cm (75in) long by 70cm (28in) wide. Make one long edge run the length of the selvage.

3 Fold under and press the selvage edge 3.25cm (1¼in) towards the wrong side of the fabric. Measure, mark, and cut a strip of 3.25cm (1¼in) fusible webbing equal to the cut length of the fabric. On the wrong side of the fabric, sandwich the webbing strip under the folded edge and press to fuse into place.

4 Fold under and press the other long edge by 6mm (¼in), then 3.25cm (1¼in) towards the wrong side of the fabric. Sandwich another webbing strip under the folded edge and press to fuse into place. (Note: If your fabric is quite thick, you may need to fuse the 6mm/¼in fold first with a strip of 6mm/¼in webbing to secure it in place, see left.)

5 Fold under and press the short ends by 1.25cm (½in), then 3.25cm (1¼in). Sandwich a piece of 6mm (¼in) fusible webbing, 5cm (2in) long at both ends of the 1.25cm (½in) fold and press to fuse into place. (Note: if your fabric is heavy, fuse a piece that runs along the entire width.) Now sandwich a strip of the 3.25cm (1¼in) fusible webbing under the wider fold and press to fuse into place.

6 Cut a strip of hook-and-loop tape, 100cm (40in) long. Separate the two strips, peel off the backing, and centre one strip 1.25cm (½in) from the folded long edge on the top side of the cover; press to fuse into place. Centre the other strip 2.5cm (1in) from the other folded hem on the wrong side of the cover; press to fuse into place.

7 Wrap the cover around the bolster form and press the strips of hook-and-loop tape to close. Cut two lengths of satin ribbon, 1m (1yd) long, angling the ends. Tie the ribbon into bows around ends of the cover to close.

Simple Bolster Cover **117**

Woven Cushion

These two-toned cushions with their neat woven pattern add punch to a neutral room. The simplest way to make woven cushion covers like these is to start with a non-fraying fabric, such as felt, faux suede, or leather. Other options include wide ribbon or twill tape. If, however, you want to use woven fabrics that complement other soft goods in your room, you can create finished strips by folding under and topstitching or hand-stitching double hems along the edges. For zing, choose fabrics or ribbons in high-contrast colours, or for a subtler look, opt for two shades of the same hue.

MATERIALS

- Ribbons, twill tape, or fabric in contrasting colours
- Lining fabric
- Square cushion pad
- Backing fabric
- Sewing kit (see pages 170–3)

Strips of vegetable-dyed linen were used to create the simple but effective woven pattern on these cushion covers and the throw on the footstool.

1 If you're using ribbon or non-fraying fabric, determine the finished width of the strips of the large-scale woven pattern by measuring the width of your cushion, adding 2.5cm (1in) and dividing the total by 5. For the smaller-scale pattern, add 2.5cm (1in) to the width of the cushion and divide by 8. If

2 Add 2.5cm (1in) to the length and width of your cushion. Then measure, mark and cut the lining and the backing fabrics to these measurements.

3 With right sides up, place strips of the same colour across the width of the lining.

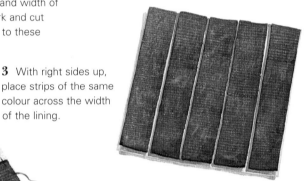

4 With right sides up, weave the contrasting strips through the first set of strips, pinning in place as you go, until the pattern is complete. Tack all around 6mm (¼in) from the perimeter, attaching the strips to the lining. Remove the pins.

you're using a woven fabric that needs to be hemmed, add 2.5cm (1in) to the width of each strip. The length of each strip should equal the length of the cushion plus 2.5cm (1in). Depending on the scale of your pattern, measure, mark and cut 5 or 8 strips from each fabric or ribbon. If you're using woven fabric, fold under and press 6mm (¼in) double hems along the long edges of each strip and hem with machine-topstitch or hand-sew with hemming stitch (see page 174).

5 With right sides facing and raw edges matching, place the woven patchwork front over the backing and pin in place. Machine-stitch the two pieces together with a 1.25cm (½in) seam all around, leaving an 20cm (8in) opening on one side. Clip the corners of the seam allowance.

6 Turn cushion cover right side out; press. Insert the cushion pad and close the opening by hand with slipstitch (see pages 173–4).

Appliqué Cushion

Very little fabric and a couple of remnants is all that's needed to create this playful accent cushion. Using a contrasting fabric to make the patchwork front of the cover produces a graphic chessboard-like pattern. You could also create a subtler look by using the same fabric for the squares and allowing the appliqué to add the decorative dash. The appliquéd images can either be drawn freehand or, if you don't feel confident of your artistic abilities, try using a stencil to create the motifs instead.

MATERIALS

- Main fabric, about 50cm (½yd)
- Secondary fabric, about 25cm (¼yd)
- Contrasting fabric remnants
- Cushion pad, 45cm (18in) square
- Sheet of fusible webbing or fabric stiffener
- Stencil (optional)
- Sewing kit (see pages 170–3)

Contrasting cotton sateen fabrics form the shell of this cushion cover and the appliquéd motifs were made from remnant scraps.

1 Measure, mark, and cut a piece of main fabric, 48cm (19in), square for the back. Measure, mark, and cut 2 pieces of main fabric, 25cm (10in) square, and 2 pieces of secondary fabric, 25cm (10in) square, for the front. Fold in and press all the edges of each piece by 1.25cm (½in) to the wrong side of the fabric, then open out the folds.

2 Press the remnants of fabric onto the fusible webbing or fabric stiffener. Hand-draw or use a stencil to create appliqué motifs on the remnants and cut them out.

3 Pin and tack one motif onto the right side of each piece of secondary fabric. Machine-sew the perimeters of the appliqués to the fabric pieces using satin stitch, or hand-sew using satin stitch or buttonhole stitch (see pages 174–5).

4 Place and pin each secondary fabric piece over the small main fabric pieces, with right sides facing and raw edges matching. Machine stitch the right-hand side of one set of pieces and the left-hand side of the other set with 1.25cm (½in) seams along the fold lines.

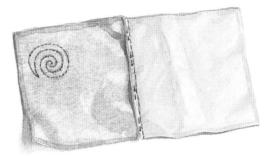

5 Open the pieces out flat, wrong side up, and press the seams.

6 Place one set of squares over the other, with right sides facing, raw edges matching and contrasting colours opposite each other. Machine-stitch the two sets together with a 1.25cm (½in) seam. Open out the front panel flat, wrong side up, and press the centre seam.

7 Place the front panel over the back, with right sides facing and raw edges matching. Machine-stitch all 4 sides with 1.25cm (½in) seams along the fold lines, leaving a 20cm (8in) opening in the middle of one side.

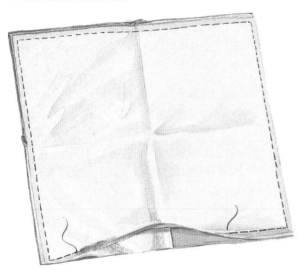

8 Clip the seam allowances at the corners, turn the cover right side out and press. Insert the cushion pad and hand-sew the opening closed neatly with slipstitch (see pages 173–4).

Shaped Chair Cushion

Whether it's sleek and modern or shapely and traditional, a dining chair becomes a lot more appealing when the seat is topped with this pretty padded cushion. A thin, tightly woven fabric, such as silk or cotton sateen, will enable you to create the spiralling pleats with the least amount of bulk. The pleated rosette at the centre works best with a lightweight fabric, too. Choose a solid or skinny-striped fabric and let the pleats grab the attention. And consider using a complementary heavier-weight fabric, such as velvet or mohair, on the flat bottom to allow the cushion to be flipped for seasonal variation.

MATERIALS
- Fabric – tight weaves and light weights work best
- Foam, 2.5cm (1in) thick
- Nylon zip, 40cm (16in) long
- Piping
- Wadding (batting) or hollow-fill polyester (optional)
- Compass or large plate
- Sewing kit (see pages 170–3)

A pretty, pleated top with a central rosette and slim piping around the gusset add decorative polish to this classy round chair cushion.

1 To determine the diameter of the cushion, measure the chair seat at the shortest width and subtract 2.5cm (1in). Use a large plate or compass to trace the diameter of the cushion onto the foam. Cut out the cushion form. (For a slightly fluffier form, cut out additional circles of wadding or add polyester hollow-fill above and below the foam when the cover is complete.)

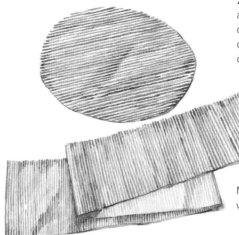

2 For the bottom of the cushion, measure, mark, and cut a piece of fabric 2.5cm (1in) larger than diameter of the foam pad all around. Machine- or hand-sew the perimeter of the bottom with overcast stitch using an edging foot, if desired (see page 178). For the top of the cushion, measure, mark and cut a piece of fabric whose length is 1⅔ of the circumference of the cushion plus 1.25cm (½in) and whose width equals the radius plus 1.25cm (½in). Note: If you need to join pieces to achieve the required length, add an extra 1.25cm (½in) for seam allowances to each piece. Machine- or hand-sew the perimeter edges with overcast stitch and edging foot, if desired.

3 Along one long edge of the cushion top fabric, fold in and pin 5cm (2in) pleats with a tuck-under about 1.2–1.25cm (⅜–½in) for each pleat. Tack along the perimeter to secure.

4 Create the round shape of the top by folding in the free ends of the pleats to overlap neatly in the centre. Overlap and tuck the short raw ends of the fabric to the back. Tack the centre pleats, then tack the short raw ends together. Machine-stitch the short raw ends to close the circle.

5 To sew the zip into the gusset: cut 2 strips of fabric 45cm (18in) long by 5cm (2in). Fold over and press one long edge of each strip by 2cm (¾in) towards the wrong side. With the zip closed, place the folded edge of one strip next to the zip teeth. Using a zipper foot (see page 178), topstitch close to the edge. Place the folded edge of the second strip just over the topstitching to conceal zip and topstitching. Guiding the zipper foot along the edge of the zip teeth, topstitch this piece in place, and stitch across the bottom and top of the zip. With the zip closed, this part of the gusset should be 5cm (2in) wide. Trim away excess fabric if necessary.

7 Cut two lengths of piping equal to the circumference of the cushion form, plus 2.5cm (1in). With raw edges matching, pin and tack the lengths of piping to the top and bottom of the gusset, overlapping the ends and folding towards the raw edge. Pin and tack the gusset to the bottom of the cushion cover, with right sides facing, raw edges matching, and the piping sandwiched between the fabric layers. Adjust the fold at the top of the zip if necessary to perfect the fit of the gusset. Machine-stitch all layers together using a piping foot (see page 178).

8 Pin and tack the pleated top of the cushion cover to the gusset, with right sides facing, raw edges matching, and piping sandwiched between the fabric layers. Adjust the pleats slightly and trim any excess fabric around the perimeter, if necessary. Machine-stitch all layers together using a piping foot. Turn the cover right side out; press or steam the pleats.

9 To make the rosette, measure, mark, and cut a strip of fabric 20cm (24in) long by 5cm (2in) wide. Fold and press the strip in half lengthwise, right sides out, then fold under and press all raw edges by 1.25cm (½in) all around; topstitch the edges to close. Fold in one short end and then turn and gradually pleat the strip into a circle, hand-sewing each of the pleats into place until the rosette is complete. Hand-sew the rosette to the centre of the top.

6 To make the remainder of the gusset, measure, mark, and cut a strip of fabric equal to the circumference of the cushion form minus 30cm (12in), by 5cm (2in). With right sides facing and raw edges matching, machine-stitch the short ends of the gusset to the top and bottom of the zip portion of the gusset with a 1.25cm (½in) seam across the top and 3.25cm (1¼in) seam across the bottom (if it's nylon, you can sew right over the bottom of the zip). Trim off the bottom of the zip by about 2cm (¾in). At one short end of the gusset, fold over about 1.25cm (½in) to cover the top of the zip when closed and pin the fold into place.

10 Insert the foam pad (and the layers of cotton wadding or hollow-fill polyester if desired) and close the zipper.

Daybed Cushion and Bolsters

Ideal for a small or dual-purpose space, such as a guest bedroom/home office, a daybed provides the perfect perch for relaxing by day or sleeping by night. Such a versatile piece of furniture is bound to get a lot of use – and is therefore very likely to need recovering quite frequently. Fortunately, sewing covers for the cushion and bolsters is fairly simple. Why not make an extra set so you can also change the look seasonally? If you make more than one set of covers, use zips for easy removal, instead of closing the cushion covers with slipstitching.

MATERIALS

- Decorative fabric (for measuring tips, see pages 179–81)
- Lining fabric or ticking (if you are using feather or down fillings this must be featherproof)
- Feathers, down, or hollow-fill polyester (or polyester foam and readymade bolster forms)
- Cord
- Circular template, such as a plate, saucer, or cup
- Compass
- Zips (optional)
- Sewing kit (see pages 170–3)

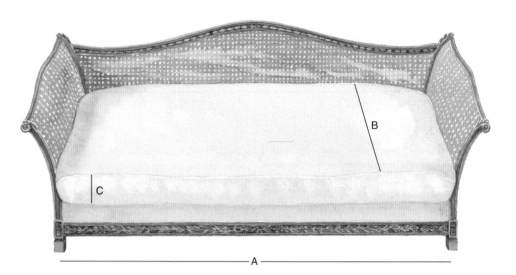

A richly striped silk-and-cotton fabric gives a luxurious softness to this Napoleonic daybed.

1 To calculate the amount of fabric you'll need for the cushion, measure the length (A), the width (B), and depth (C) of the cushion, and add 2.5cm (1in) to each measurement for seam allowances. For the top and bottom, you'll need two pieces that are A by B plus seam allowance. For the gusset, you'll need one piece that is C by A + A + B+ B plus seam allowance. If you need more than one fabric width to cover the length of the cushion, plan to use one width in the middle and join a half width or less on either side to achieve the desired size, factoring in the size of the repeat when calculating fabric quantities (see pages 165–6).

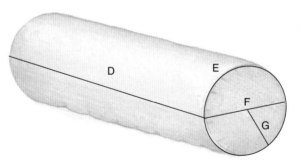

2 To calculate the amount of fabric for each bolster, measure the length (D) by the circumference (E), then add the circumference (E) by the radius (G) of the circular end for the gathered end piece, and then add 2.5cm (1in) to each dimension for seam allowances.

3 Cut out the cushion cover and lining. Making sure that the grain is straight and the pattern is square, measure, mark, and cut 2 fabric pieces for the top and bottom of the cushion (A by B plus seam allowances) from both fabrics. Using the saucer or cup as a guide, mark a rounded edge at each corner of each piece of both fabrics and cut to round off the corners. Measure, mark, and cut the cushion gusset (C by A + A + B+ B plus seam allowance) from both fabrics. (Remember to factor in seam allowances for all joins to achieve the required length.)

4 Measure, mark, and cut 2 pieces for the bolster cover and casing (D by E plus seam allowances) from both fabrics. Measure, mark, and cut 2 decorative fabric pieces (E by G plus seam allowances) for the gathered end pieces of each bolster – 4 in total.

5 Using a compass, draw a circle measuring the diameter (F) plus 2.5cm (1in) on the pattern paper. Pin the pattern to the lining fabric and cut out 2 pieces for the ends of the casing for each bolster – 4 in total.

6 To make the bolster covers, fold the fabric pieces (D by E) in half crosswise with right sides facing and raw edges matching. Pin, tack and machine-stitch the long edge together, leaving a 15–25cm (6–10in) gap in the middle, or enough room to be able to insert the bolster form. (To include a zip, see step 5 of the Shaped Chair Cushion, pages 122–3.) Press open the seams.

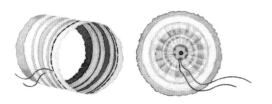

7 To make the gathered end pieces, fold the oblong pieces of fabric (E by G) in half crosswise with right sides facing and raw edges matching. Pin, tack, and machine-stitch the short sides together to form small cylinders. Run a strong piece of thread along one side edge, 6mm (¼in) from the edge, using running stitch (see page 173). Pull the ends of the thread to form a gathered circle, then tie the ends of the thread tightly and secure with a few hand stitches at the back. With right sides facing and raw edges matching, pin, tack, and machine-stitch each end piece to each cylinder of the decorative fabric. Cut notches into the seam allowances to allow a smooth fit, then turn the covers right side out.

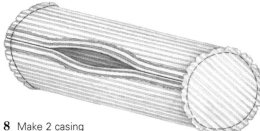

8 Make 2 casing covers for the bolsters, as in step 6. With right sides facing and raw edges matching, pin, tack, and machine-stitch the circular end pieces to the cylinders. Cut notches into the seam allowances, and turn the casings right side out. Insert the filling and slipstitch the opening in the side seam closed (see page 173–4).

9 Fold the gusset in half crosswise, with right sides facing and raw edges matching. Pin and machine-stitch the short ends together to form one large loop; press open the seams.

10 To make the cushion cover, pin the top piece to the gusset with right sides together and patterns aligned. Position the gusset seams at the back or at the sides. Tack, then machine-stitch the 2 pieces together, easing the gusset around the corners. Cut notches into the seam allowances around the corners. Repeat to attach the bottom piece the same way, leaving an opening along the back to insert the foam, pad, or filling. Turn the cover right side out through the gap in the seam. (To include a zip, see step 5 for the Shaped Chair Cushion, pages 122–3.)

11 Repeat steps 9 and 10 using the lining fabric to make the cushion casing. To avoid bulk, make sure the seam allowances do not fall in the same place as those in the top cover. Insert the foam or filling into the casing and slipstitch the opening closed. Insert the filled casing into the cover and slipstitch or zip closed.

12 Using matching thread, attach the cord to the seams at the top and bottom of the cushion cover and at the ends of the bolster covers sewing small stitches unobtrusively through the cord and the fabric at the seam. Join the cord at the back: unravel the strands at each end just a little, then intertwine them and hand-sew them together neatly.

covers

Like a well-made dress, an attractive fabric cover brings out the best in a piece of furniture with great bones, or hides a multitude of flaws in one that has passed the point of shabby chic. Aside from protecting surfaces from wear and tear or extending the life of your furnishings, fabric covers – from tablecloths and bedspreads to lampshades and loose covers – also allow you to give your decor an occasional lift to reflect changes in your taste or the seasons. Think of the mood-brightening effect of a cheerful checked tablecloth on a worn farm table or the transformative power that a white canvas loose cover can have when fitted over a velvet-upholstered armchair or sofa. Whether formal and fitted or casual and loose, covers can be made of any type of fabric – from lustrous silks and cotton damasks, which are pricey and need careful treatment, to printed cotton canvases, which are durable and easy to look after – depending on their intended purpose – the projects on pages 140–59 will give plenty of inspiration. And covers made from fade- and stain-resistant synthetic fabrics can add comfort and practicality to outdoor settings, too.

keeping it UNDER WRAPS

Providing beauty as well as function, a well-made fabric cover does double-duty in any room. Made from a lovely damask and trimmed with a bullion fringe, a pretty tablecloth can turn a hall table into a decorative focal point. But it also transforms the table into a practical storage area by hiding baskets, boots, and umbrellas beneath it. By the same token, a loose chair cover made from brightly coloured cotton and edged with a flirty ruffled skirt gives an old side chair a new lease of life. It might also link the chair with furnishings covered in the same fabric, giving a motley collection of sofas and chairs a unified look. Sideboards, consoles, and shelving units, ottomans, armchairs, and sofas can all be updated and refreshed with a custom-made cover.

left Topped with a loose cover in a neutral cotton, an upholstered chair receives a casual summer look.
above Old, white-painted furniture and a modern retro fabric are paired to great effect.

Tablecloths

Whether it's a Sunday breakfast in the country, an alfresco lunch on a terrace, or a fancy dinner party in a formal dining room, any meal is more appealing when served on a table dressed with a pretty tablecloth. Although readymade table linens come in a wide array of colours and printed patterns, customized tablecloths are relatively easy to create, and afford you the opportunity to link your table with other soft furnishings, such as curtains, chair cushions, or loose covers.

Making your own dining tablecloths also allows you to instantly change the mood of a room for special occasions or holidays. Layered over a floor-length natural linen tablecloth, a vintage paisley in the rich red, pale olive, and burnt orange colours of fallen leaves could be used to warm up a table for an autumn gathering, and an embroidered and beaded velvet runner can add richness and sparkle to a Christmas table. Swathed in dreamy chiffon, the same table can take on a completely different look for a wedding breakfast or on Mother's day, while a sari could be used to give it an exotic flavour for an Asian-inspired dinner party.

Tablecloths can also dress up or dress down a table. A fitted floor-length custom tablecloth with crisp box pleats and flourishes of ornamental trim will give an ordinary table an air of formality (see pages 154–5); or you can brighten a table for everyday meals by using a readymade tablecloth simply embellished with rick rack or by making one from a cheerful check and adding scalloped edges (see pages 142–3).

Outdoor dining tables and chairs are ideal for taking chances with bold colours or patterns. They lend themselves to creative tablecloths for different kinds of meals or styles of entertaining. A blue-and-white striped fabric embroidered with anchors or other nautical motifs would make a great accompaniment to a seafood supper for example, and could be paired with simple-to-make matching outdoor chair covers (see pages 140–1).

Over the centuries, the use of fabric tablecloths has also extended well beyond the dining room. From the silk-draped dressing tables in the Rococo rooms of 18th-century French houses to the carpet-covered occasional tables and sideboards of the Victorian era

above A large-scale checked fabric provides a vibrant contrast to dining chairs covered in a pretty *toile de Jouy* and links in with other red-checked fabrics in the kitchen beyond.
left A tablecloth made of red-and-white checked fabric and rough beige linen lends hand-crafted charm to this casual dining table.

top left Covered with a fitted cloth that has a ruffled border, an outdoor table becomes the fanciful centrepiece for an alfresco brunch.

top right A vintage American checked tablecloth, bandana-inspired napkins, and spongeware crockery merge in a two-toned scheme.

above A patchwork of yellow-and-white poplin squares makes a bright cover for a round table.

opposite Fabrics in a variety of stripes and checks prevent the extensive use of red becoming overwhelming.

to the trimmed and tailored covers used on hall tables today, decorative tablecloths have long been employed to bring a touch of softness to every kind of table in every room. They are also wonderful easy-to-change decorative elements that can inject personality into spaces to give them a low-cost lift.

Tables of all shapes and sizes are candidates. Covered with a brightly patterned chintz or silk taffeta, a small, undistinguished round table can become an attention-grabbing focal point, introducing a shot of colour or touch of luxury into a living room. An old bedside table can coordinate with new linens when topped with a fabric in a matching colour or complementary pattern. Or, hidden under a floor-length cover, even a small desk table can serve double-duty and be pressed into service as a serving station or mini buffet table in a dining room.

Fabrics and Finishing Touches

Prone as they are to spots and stains, dining tablecloths for daily use are best made from cotton or linen fabrics, as these are easiest to

clean and can be machine-washed. Since they are used less frequently, table linens intended only for festive occasions can be made from decorative fabrics that should be dry-cleaned only. Upbeat checks or lively stripes, graphic vine-like florals, pretty and practical poly-silks, and retro prints or vintage fabrics are ideal for everyday tablecloths or runners, while a Fortuny-style fabric, a silk damask, or a vibrant Asian print could be used to make a tablecloth for special occasions.

Decorative tablecloths in living rooms and bedrooms especially lend themselves to fabrics that provide decorator polish. For these tablecloths, you might opt for pretty cotton prints or stripes for casual rooms and luxurious silks or embroidered textiles for more formal spaces.

Any table cover is even more appealing when embellished with personalized touches or decorative details. For dining tablecloths, consider scalloped borders, ribbon trim, cross-stitched motifs, or embroidered monograms. You might finish the hem of round bedside table cover with fringe or thick contrasting piping to call attention to its sweeping lines and add a sensuous grace note. And grosgrain ribbon, contrasting banding, or braid could add a touch of refinement to a tailored tablecloth with crisp pleats topping a console or a hall table.

When designing your own dining table linens, bear in mind that the standard height of a dining table is 72cm (29in) and that the overhang of a tablecloth should be at least 30cm (12in) all around. If you're covering a table in a living room, entrance hall, or bedroom with a fragile or precious fabric, such as embroidered silk or taffeta, consider having a piece of glass, 0.75–1.25cm ($\frac{1}{4}$–$\frac{1}{2}$in) thick, cut to fit the tabletop to protect the fabric from spills or other damage.

Loose Covers

Ever since the 17th century, when furniture makers began the practice of supplying lighter-weight, less-expensive fabric covers along with fine-quality upholstered seating, loose covers have provided an appealing and affordable way to both preserve expensive upholstery fabric and change the spirit of a room.

Like jeans and a T-shirt on a well-toned body, cotton canvas or denim loose covers give fine upholstered seating a relaxed quality during the summer months when formality takes a back seat. They also extend the life of upholstered pieces, protecting costly upholstery fabric from the ravages of everyday use. By warding off the harmful fading rays of the sun, loose covers also keep upholstery fabrics looking fresher longer.

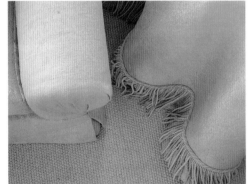

top and inset In a creamy room, a printed linen tablecloth with a thick cotton fringe provides an ornate contrast.
above A deep bullion fringe gives classic decorative polish to an elegant silk tablecloth on an occasional table.
right On a console table, a bold red-checked tablecloth is bordered in a smaller-scale check, highlighting the kick pleats.
far right A panel of heavily embroidered antique peasant linen forms the inset top of a cover for a low ottoman.

Decorative touches

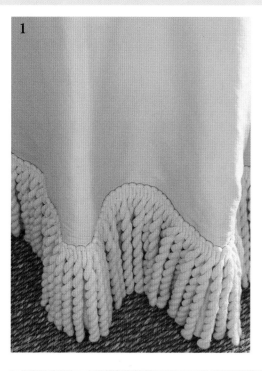

1 Fringed edges

A mercerized cotton bullion fringe on a tablecloth provides texture and interest. Fringing, which is easily attached to both readymade covers and custom-made ones, is a quick and easy way to personalize such items.

2 Tied pleats

Neat box pleats are given a boost with the addition of simple tiebacks on the corners of this fitted table cover. The plain texture and colour of the cover lends itself to embellishment with subtly coloured tiebacks or even stronger colours to provide splashes of interest.

SEE **PAGES 154–5 FOR MAKING BOX PLEATS**

3 Loose with colourful edges

The red-checked border on this heavy matelassé table cover creates a colourful highlight in the corner of a room. As with fringes, borders like this can be added to most table covers. They can be matching or contrasting, depending on the effect desired.

SEE **PAGES 142–3 FOR ADDING BORDERS**

4 Pleated edging

Red piping and a red ribbon hem draws attention to the pleated skirt on this chair cover. Pleats require careful measuring and folding to ensure uniformity of size around a piece of furniture.

SEE **PAGES 146–7 FOR MAKING PIPING**

right Casual cotton loose covers unify disparate upholstered pieces and give them a relaxed look for the summer.
far right An antique chair gets a new lease of life with a loose cover in cotton ticking and cheery ties of red binding tape.
below Covered in a fresh white cotton loose cover, a shapely vintage chair lives contentedly in a contemporary context.
opposite Dark blue linen panels edged with a checked trim are tied to an antique armchair giving it a fresh flavour.

Any kind of seating benefits from the second skin a loose cover can provide. Full-skirted covers adorned with voluminous bows may be used to dress up a set of upholstered dining chairs. Or loose covers made from a simple ticking stripe or colourful patterned cotton can give a set of living room furnishings a casual look during the warm weather seasons. A loose cover made from a pretty floral print brings a feminine touch to a straight-backed wooden side chair, while a solid-coloured cover with a contrasting piping can give an old bedroom chair a brand-new look.

Choosing Fabrics

Although it is possible to make a cover from velvet, loose-cover makers and fabric manufacturers recommend using it only for very tight-fitted covers on linear upholstered pieces, such as daybed cushions. Also avoid loosely woven textiles or delicate fabrics, such as taffetas and pure silks, as they lack durability (silks may be used to make covers as a decorative statement on occasional chairs that are rarely used, however). Instead, opt for lighter-weight fabrics, such as ticking, gingham, or cotton canvas (see pages 152–3). For wooden chairs or padded dining chairs, printed cotton, quilted fabrics, or chintz make wonderful loose covers. In living rooms or family rooms, where upholstered pieces are subject to steady use and predisposed to spills and stains, a more durable, low-maintenance fabric is the best choice.

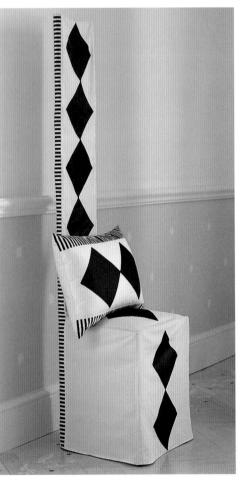

top A cheerful blue-and-white checked fitted cover updates an upholstered armchair. The cushions and side seams are edged with contrasting piping.
above A collection of contemporary armchairs gets a softer look with skirted, cream damask loose covers, complete with neat kick pleats.
right This loose cover with its contrasting cotton appliqué diamonds highlights the unusual proportions of a Charles Rennie Mackintosh-style chair.

Consider twill, denim, or cotton canvas. Remember, though, that heavier fabrics are generally more difficult to work with as loose covers often include several layers of overlapping seams, which can be tough for a sewing machine needle to drive through. Linen, though it wrinkles easily, feels cool next to the skin and can be great for casual environments, such as country homes or seaside houses. It's also possible to use dressmaking fabrics for loose covers if you don't expect them to last long. If you do use such a fabric, sew on or apply a fusible backing to make it more durable.

Colours, Patterns, and Details

If you are interested in making covers for several disparate pieces of seating in a room, crafting all of them from the same fabric can be a way to unify them. You might also choose fabrics that share the same colour but vary in tonal value or texture, such as pairing a taupe linen for chairs with a cream matelassé for a sofa, for example. Creating loose covers from completely different fabrics – a solid for a sofa, stripes for armchairs, and a floral for a side chair, for example – will generate a more complex and interesting composition. The important thing to remember if you opt for this approach is to link the fabrics by choosing those with colours in the same palette. Including fabrics in a mix of large-, medium- and small-scale patterns will also keep the overall picture balanced.

When choosing fabrics, always bear in mind both the character of the setting, the style of your furnishings, and the effect you hope to achieve. Do you want to reinforce a feeling of formality in a traditional room with antique furnishings? Or do you want inject the same room and furnishings with a more relaxed or contemporary flavour? If you want to create covers from patterned fabrics, remember, too, that the style and scale of the pattern needs to relate not only to the style of the piece of furniture but also to its size and proportions (see pages 158–9). Patterned fabrics will also need to be matched from one section of the chair to other, while napped fabrics need to be cut so that the nap runs in the same direction on all sides. (For information on matching patterns and ensuring your covers fit well, see page 180.)

Sofa and chair covers

1 Simple Loose Covers

Cheerful table napkins can be easily converted into vibrant tie-on covers for outdoor café-style chairs. In fact, any remnants of fabric would make an attractive cover and ribbons or fabric tape could be used for the ties.

SEE FOLDING CHAIR COVER, PAGES 140–1

SEE PAGE 157, STEPS 11 AND 12, FOR MAKING TIES IN MATCHING FABRIC

2 Formal Loose Covers

A woven floral jacquard fabric has been used to create a loose cover for a dining chair to complement curtains and blinds. Loose covers can be made for a wide variety of chairs and they don't need to be closely fitted to be effective.

SEE SUNFLOWER APPLIQUÉ CHAIR COVER, PAGES 152–3
OCCASIONAL CHAIR COVER, PAGES 156–7

3 Fitted Furniture Covers

Knotted ties fasten the back of a loose cover on a slope-backed chair and call attention to the edges of the piped skirted panels. This is a semi-fitted cover that suits the informal setting of this room, even so care needs to be taken when making this type of cover that the fabric pattern matches across the back and arms and the fit is neat and close in these areas too.

SEE FITTED WINGCHAIR COVER, PAGES 158–61

above A blue-and-white cover softens a baby's cot and matches the curtains.
right Monogrammed tie-on loose covers give an iron bedstead a welcoming look in a cosy cottage bedroom.
below This elaborately shaped headboard was heavily padded then topped with a tight piped cover in a checked cotton.

Thoughtful extras give loose covers a sense of refinement that elevates them from shapeless protective coverings to ambience-altering decorative elements. While appliqué is one way to add style (see pages 152–3), breezy ruffles (see pages 156–7), tailored skirts, soft bow enclosures, crisp ties, or covered buttons work harder to bring out the best in the personality of a chair – or change it altogether.

Covers for Other Furnishings

The same practical and aesthetic benefits that fabric covers offer to wooden or upholstered seating can be easily applied to other upholstered or hard

furnishings. Fitted fabric coverings can refresh upholstered headboards (see pages 148–9), protect a sideboard from scratches and spills, or transform the character of a wooden bench or stool (see pages 146–7). Custom bed coverings – such as duvet covers, bedspreads (see pages 144–5), coverlets, and dust ruffles – can give a bedroom a seasonal change of scene. And coverings for framed elements, like lampshades or freestanding shelving units, can shield light, hide clothing or toys, and provide protection from sun.

As with custom tablecloths and loose covers for chairs, choosing a fabric that is appropriate for the context and suitable to the style of the surroundings is key to a successful outcome. Using a pretty blue-and-white *toile de Jouy* as a headboard cover is a classic way to brighten a guest bedroom and can provide the starting

point for a soothing new colour scheme. Creating a
cupboard cover from a cheerful awning stripe, on the
other hand, can add zest to a child's room and play
off other patterned soft furnishings in the room (see
pages 150–1). Trims and decorative closures, such as
contrasting piping, scalloped borders, button tabs, or
bow ties, bring inspired finishing touches to these
fabric covers, too.

far left A pretty *toile de Jouy*
fabric covers a padded folding
screen and makes a pleasing
partnership with the larger scale
wallpaper in matching tones.
left Gathered blue-and-white
gingham panels mounted inside
the glazed doors of a wall-
mounted cabinet conceal the
crockery stowed within.

Practical Considerations

Part of the appeal of any fabric cover is its ability to
be easily removed for cleaning. Although many fabrics
can be machine-washed and dried, most decorator
fabrics are treated with a finish or sizing, which may
resist stains, keep the fabric crisp, provide lustre or
protect the fabric from fading, and should therefore
should be dry cleaned only.

Even if your fabric is machine-washable, repeated
washings can also cause stress to the seams as well as
the fabric fibres, so dry cleaning is the best way to clean
many covers to preserve the integrity of their fabric as
well as their construction. If you plan to your launder
your fabric covers in a washing machine, be sure to
choose a fabric that is machine-washable.

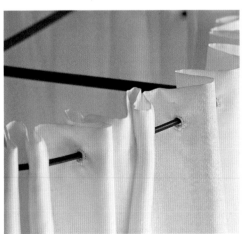

above Lampshades with a
candystripe bias-cut edging (left),
gathered under a band of gimp
(centre), and with box-pleats and
a shell fringe (right) personalize
a variety of light fixtures.
left A soft creamy fabric pierced
with eyelets and threaded onto
a lampshade frame, gives an
arty look to a lamp in an urban
loft space.

Folding-chair Cover

These simple chair covers are easy to make using squares of fabric or hemmed napkins and are quick to remove for storage or cleaning. Use durable, colourfast outdoor fabric for these cheerful covers to ensure that they will survive several seasons. Cotton canvas, sailcloth, or twill make good choices, too. Bright solid colours look their best in strong sunlight; for a more lively overall effect choose graphic prints, such as vibrant paisleys, bold stripes, or casual woven ikat patterns. Or mix and match for a more informal ambience.

MATERIALS

- Fabric – hemmed napkins, 5cm (2in) larger than chair seat all around or use squares of outdoor fabric (for measuring tips, see pages 179–81)
- Cotton twill tape, 2.5cm (1in) wide for ties
- Thin foam padding about 1.25–2.5cm (½–1in) thick
- Sewing kit (see pages 170–3)

An alfresco meal becomes more festive when the table and chairs are dressed up for the occasion. This blue-striped fabric is crisp but informal.

1 If you're using fabric for your covers (rather than finished napkins), measure the chair seat, and add 15cm (6in) to each of the dimensions. Measure, mark, and cut 3 pieces of fabric to these dimensions. Fold, press, and pin 1.25cm (½in) double hems all the way around each piece, then machine-topstitch the hems in place. On one piece of hemmed fabric or napkin, mark the positions of 2 buttonholes 2.5cm (1in) from one end of the fabric and 2.5cm (1in) from each side. Using a buttonhole foot (see page 178), machine-stitch buttonholes, and cut slits in the holes, or cut slits and hand-stitch buttonholes (see page 174).

2 Measure and cut 4 strips of twill tape, each 50cm (20in) long. Pin two pieces of tape to the wrong side of the fabric near the corners opposite the buttonholes, 2.5cm (1in) from each edge, so that they align with the buttonholes when the fabric is folded in half. (The free ends of the tape should face out to the sides). Machine-stitch the tape to the fabric making a small square shape. Pin two lengths of the fabric in the same manner to the right side, covering the stitched squares, and sew the tape to the fabric, again making a small square shape. Hand-hem the loose ends.

3 Press the cover flat, then fold it, right side out, over the back of the chair.

5 Place the foam pad on the chair seat and mark the points where it meets the back chair legs. Place one of the remaining hemmed fabric pieces (or napkins) wrong side up on a work surface and position the foam pad on top, centring it within the four sides. This piece will make the bottom of the chair cover.

6 Measure and cut 4 more lengths of twill tape each 50cm (20in) long. Position 2 lengths of tape above and below the pad on each side. Align them with the chair-leg marks on the foam pad and make sure each overlaps the pad by about 5cm (2in). Pin and loosely stitch the tape to the pad and bottom cover.

7 Place the other hemmed fabric piece or napkin, right side up, on top of the pad, aligning the edges with the bottom cover, and pin. Machine-topstitch around all four sides, securing the twill tape ties between the seams. Finish the tie ends as in step 2.

4 Pull the ties through the buttonholes and tie in bows to secure the cover to the chair top.

8 Place the finished cushion on the seat and fasten the tapes to the chair legs to secure it in place. Finish the ties with bows to match the chair back cover.

Folding-chair Cover **141**

Scalloped-border Tablecloth

This casual tablecloth is edged with a pretty scalloped border and adds charm to a breakfast nook or kitchen dining area. Choose a white, ecru, or ivory cotton or linen for the main fabric to keep the look classic and clean. Make the border in a fabric with colours or patterns that complement other soft furnishings in the room while adding zest to the tablecloth. For a personal finishing touch, add a monogram – embroidered by machine or by hand – to one side of the tablecloth.

MATERIALS

- Main fabric for tablecloth
- Contrasting fabric for border (for measuring tips, see pages 179–81)
- Circular template for scallops, such as a plate, saucer, or cup
- Sewing kit (see pages 170–3)

A contrasting scalloped border adds personality to a simple tablecloth. The cover-up is ideal for casual dining areas, and hides dents and scratches in a weathered table.

1 Measure the length and width of the tabletop and add the desired drop, including the border. Double the drop and add this figure to your width and length dimensions. Measure the diameter of your scallop template, and divide the length and width measurements by this figure, rounding up or down to the nearest whole number. This determines the number of scallops on the long and short sides.

2 To determine the finished length and width the border needs to be to accommodate complete scallops at each corner, multiply the diameter of your template by the number of scallops for each side. To determine the cut length of each border piece, multiply the diameter of your template by the number of scallops for each side and add twice the diameter of the template plus 2.5cm (1in). To determine the cut width, double the diameter of the template and add 7.5cm (3in). Using these measurements, mark and cut a piece of border fabric for each side. Fold the material in half lengthwise, right sides facing and patterns matching, then pin. Using a fabric marker and ruler, draw a line along the middle of the length of the folded fabric.

3 Using your template, mark the outline of the scallops. Centre the template over the marked line, and starting 1.25cm (½in) from one short end, draw a ¾ scallop, then continue moving the template and marking ½ scallops until you reach the opposite end; end with a ¾ scallop, 1.25cm (½in) from the end of the fabric. This is your stitching (or trace) line. Repeat for the three remaining border pieces.

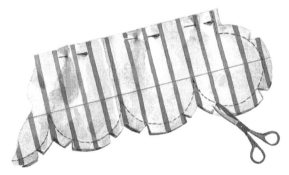

4 Pin the fabric pieces for each separate border, and machine-sew along the stitching lines. Cut out the scallops leaving 1.25cm (½in) from your stitching line. Clip fabric at intervals along the curved edges so it will lie flat when turned right side out.

5 Turn each border right side out and press flat with an iron.

6 To join the four sides of the border, mitre the corners by folding and pressing the ¾ scallops in half along the diagonal. Tuck the excess fabric inside the end of the border, making sure the patterns align. Press. Machine-topstitch the straight edges of the mitred corners together or hand-sew using slipstitch (see page 176). When all four corners are joined, clip excess fabric inside corners. Press again.

7 Turn under 1.25cm (½in) on the raw edges of the long and short sides; press. Measure the straight long and short edges of the border; add 1.25cm (½in) to each dimension. Measure, mark, and cut the main tablecloth fabric using these dimensions. Slip the tablecloth fabric between the turned-under border edges and pin and tack around all four sides. Attach the border to the cloth using machine-topstitch or hand hemming stitch (see page 174). Press again.

Tea-towel Bedspread

With their appealing patterns and designs and variety of interesting weaves, tea towels have long served as pretty and practical accessories in the kitchen. But their affordable price and large size makes them ideal for other uses too. Trimmed of their borders and pieced together in a grid, a selection of tea towels has been used to make this lovely reversible bedspread. There are beautiful examples of tea towels – some, woven on antique jacquard looms, look as if they should be framed, others celebrate aspects of French or English culture or history in glorious colour. Many are also embellished with pretty embroidered motifs. The best tea towels for this project are those with repeating patterns, such as plaids, stripes, or checks, but a mix of embroidered or cross-stitched tea towels would work beautifully too.

MATERIALS

For a 1.5m (5ft) queen-size bed:

- 15 standard-size tea towels (for measuring tips, see pages 179–81)
- Interlining fabric
- Contrasting fabric for backing, edging, and bows
- Sewing kit (see pages 170–3)

Sewn together in a grid and decorated with a contrasting border and bows, a collection of tea towels forms the top of a fresh, pretty bedspread.

1 Carefully cut off all the hems of the tea towels. On a work surface, place three towels face down, short edges aligned, in a row.

2 With right sides together, pin the short edges of two towels together and sew with a 1.25cm (½in) seam, making sure the patterns align. Repeat to join the free short end of the middle towel to the third towel.

3 Repeat steps 1 and 2 to make four more strips of tea towels. Align two strips, right sides facing; pin along one long edge and sew with a 1.25cm (½in) seam. Repeat with the remaining strips to complete the bedspread top. Press all seams open and flat.

4 Measure the bedspread top. Measure, mark, and cut a piece of interlining fabric to these dimensions. If you need to join fabric to achieve the correct size, overlap widths by 1.25cm (½in) and join them by machine with zigzag stitch, or by hand with herringbone stitch (see page 174) to achieve a flat seam.

5 On a work surface, lay the bedspread top right side down and place the interlining on top. Join the two layers by hand with loose running stitch (see page 174), along the tea towel seam lines, then all around the perimeter 6mm (¼in) from the edges.

6 Machine-topstitch along the stitching lines between the seams of the tea towels on the right side, leaving the running stitches intact. Do not machine-sew around the perimeter.

9 Place the bedspread right side up on a work surface. Position and pin the border to the perimeter of the bedspread, raw edges aligned. Machine-stitch the border to the bedspread with a 6mm (¼in) seam.

10 Measure, mark, and cut a piece of backing fabric, making it the same size as the bedspread. Join widths if necessary with 1.25cm (½in) seams, pressing them open and flat. Place the backing over the bedspread, right sides facing, raw edges matching, sandwiching the ruffled border between the layers. Pin and loosely stitch all around. Machine-sew with 1.25cm (½in) seams, leaving a 10in (25cm) opening on one short end. Turn the bedspread right side out, and slipstitch (see pages 173–4) the opening closed by hand.

11 Make bows for the intersections of the tea towels. Measure, mark, and prepare sixteen 12.5cm (5in) by 2.5cm (1in) strips of contrasting fabric, cut on the bias (see page 176–7). Fold and press each strip in half lengthwise, right sides facing. Machine-sew along raw edges with 6mm (¼in) seams. Turn right sides out, using the blunt end of a pencil; press flat. Fold each strip into a bow, overlapping and folding under the raw edges, then join two bows together to form a cross. Hand-sew the bows to the junctions of the towels; take the needle through the lining and backing to secure all layers.

7 To make the ruffled border, measure the perimeter of the bedspread. Cut enough 5cm (2in) strips of contrasting fabric to equal twice this perimeter measurement. Join the strips with 6mm (¼in) seams, then press open and flat. Fold the joined strip in half lengthwise, right side out, and press again.

8 Join the raw edges with running stitch (see page 173). Pull the ends of the running stitch thread to gather the fabric until the strip is the same length as the perimeter of the bedspread.

Tea-towel Bedspread **145**

Bathroom Stool Cover

A round, wooden stool that is already padded is ideal for this project, but you could add padding to the top of any stool. Choose chintz or cotton sateen fabric for a touch of luxury, or consider a solid-coloured fabric or one with a striped pattern for a contemporary look; for a country-style bathroom, try a pretty toile or fresh floral fabric. Contrasting piping around the cushion edge and skirt hem adds polish. This cover is not removable, so when complete use stain-resistant spray to protect the fabric from spills and dirt.

MATERIALS

- Round padded stool
- Main fabric (for measuring tips, see pages 179–81)
- Contrasting fabric for piping
- Piping cord
- Staple gun and staples
- Sewing kit (see pages 170–3)

If you don't have a padded stool, you can make one by covering a wooden stool seat with a piece of foam, cut to fit and fixed to the top with spray adhesive. For extra cushioning, cut and staple a layer of padding on top of this. You will need:

- Foam padding 5cm (2in) thick
- Spray adhesive
- Padding such as cotton, wool, or synthetic quilt lining (optional)

When topped with carefully chosen fabric, an ordinary wooden stool becomes a pretty seat, adding class to a bathroom or dressing area.

1 Place the fabric face down on a work surface, then lay the stool face down on the fabric, centred over the pattern repeat. Trace around the stool. Draw another circle 5cm (2in) outside the first. Cut out the fabric using the outer line.

2 Centre the fabric face up over the stool and attach it to the wood frame using the staple gun. Put in one staple, stretch the fabric taut and put in another staple on the opposite side. Repeat, starting halfway between the two staples, then stretching and stapling the opposite side; continue until complete.

3 Calculate the skirt fabric. First measure the height of the stool from the floor to the seat and add 2.5cm (1in). Then measure the circumference of the stool and double this measurement. Measure, mark, and cut a piece of fabric to these dimensions for the skirt, making sure the pattern is centred.

4 Fold the fabric in half, right sides together – matching raw edges – and sew the short sides together with a 1.25cm (½in) seam. Press the seam open. Hand-sew two rows of long running stitches (see page 173), 1.25cm (½in) in along one long edge; leave long tails of thread.

5 Make two lengths of corded piping (see pages 176–7) using the contrasting fabric. One length should be 2.5cm (1in) longer than the circumference of the stool seat, the other should be 2.5cm (1in) longer than the circumference of the skirt bottom.

6 With right sides facing and raw edges matching, pin and hand-sew the longer piping to the bottom of the skirt with long running stitch. Using a zipper foot, machine-stitch the piping 1.25cm (½in) from the raw edges. Cut excess cord, fold over and overlap the ends of the piping to cover the cord (see page 177); hand-sew in place.

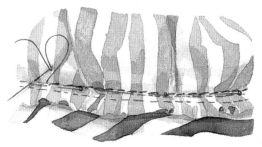

7 Turn the skirt wrong side out and press the seam allowance up towards the inside of the skirt. Neaten raw edges by machine with zigzag or overlock stitch, or overlock by hand (see page 175). Pull the two threads of the running stitches to gather the top edge of the skirt until it fits the stool seat precisely.

8 Turn the skirt right side out, and with right sides facing and raw edges matching, pin and tack the shorter piping to the top of the skirt. Using a zipper foot, machine-stitch the piping to the skirt 1.25cm (½in) from the raw edges. Cut the excess cord; fold over and overlap the ends of the piping to cover the cord; hand-sew in place.

9 With right sides facing, and raw edges facing down, slide the top of the skirt over the stool seat. Secure the gathered skirt to the stool top by pinning it evenly in place all the way around, just above the staples.

10 Use tight running stitch to hand-sew the gathered skirt to the seam allowance of the top of the stool seat just below the piping, so that the cord is positioned neatly between the rim of the seat and the skirt top.

11 Fold down the skirt cover and steam out wrinkles with a handheld steamer.

Bathroom Stool Cover **147**

Bedhead Loose Cover

This cover will refresh an upholstered headboard or brighten a wooden one. You can even make your own headboard. You will need basic woodcutting skills for a shaped board, but most timber yards will make straight cuts for a small fee. A medium-weight cotton canvas is ideal for the cover. The appliqué decoration is added for a charming finishing touch.

MATERIALS

- Shaped or upholstered headboard
- Fabric for cover (for measuring tips, see pages 179–81)
- Contrasting fabric for appliqué
- Fusible webbing or an iron-on fabric stiffener
- Piping cord
- Sewing kit (see pages 170–3)

To make your own headboard use a jigsaw to cut out the shape from plywood or medium density fibreboard (MDF). Cut some foam to the same shape and fix to the board with spray adhesive. Cover the foam with a layer of quilting and staple in place. If required, cut and nail 5 by 7.5cm (2 by 4in) battens to the back of the headboard to raise it to the desired height. You will need:

- Plywood or MDF and battens
- Roll of foam 5cm (2in) thick
- Padding such as cotton, wool, or synthetic quilt lining (optional)
- Jigsaw
- Staple gun and staples
- Spray adhesive

Embellish the loose cover with appliqué to produce a customized headboard; alternatively, try making an embroidered monogram or floral motif.

1 Lay the headboard on pattern paper and trace around it. Draw another line 1.25cm (½in) outside the trace line and cut out your pattern along this line. Fold the fabric in half, then pin the pattern to the fabric. Cut out two pieces of fabric, one for the back and one for the front. You may need to take pieces of fabric from both sides of the selvage to achieve the necessary width before you cut the pattern (see Fabric widths, page 166).

2 To determine the length of the gusset, measure along the sides and top of the cover. To determine the width of the gusset, measure the depth of the headboard and add 2.5cm (1in) for the seam allowance. Measure, mark, and cut a piece of fabric to these dimensions, piecing fabric, if necessary, to achieve the desired length.

3 Using the main fabric, make up two lengths of corded piping, both equal to the entire length of the gusset (see pages 176–7).

4 For the appliqué motif, iron a 25cm (10in) square of contrasting fabric onto fusible webbing or fabric stiffener. Draw the star shape, about 20cm (8in) high, on pattern paper and cut it out. Pin this pattern onto the fabric and cut around the shape.

5 Centre the top of the star about 6.25cm (2½in) from the top of the piece of fabric that will make the front of the cover. Pin it in place, then machine- or hand-sew it to the cover with satin stitch (see page 174).

6 Make the cover. With right sides facing and raw edges matching, sandwich the piping between gusset and front cover. Pin, then stitch with long running stitches (see page 174). Using a zipper foot, machine-stitch all layers together with a 1.25cm (½in) seam, see left. Repeat to join the gusset and the other strip of piping to the cover back, see below left. Turn right side out.

7 Fold, press, and pin a 1.25cm (½in) double hem along the bottom of the cover. Machine-topstitch in place. Press cover and fit it over the headboard.

Fabric-covered Cupboard

This mundane freestanding shelving unit has been transformed into an appealing and decorative piece of furniture using a swathe of fabric. Ideal for a child's room, fabric-covered shelves in wood or metal are great for concealing clothes, books, or toys. This cupboard is trimmed with a matching ribbon and a scalloped border, but you could use a contrasting colour. Enhance the room's decor by playing off your colour choice against other shades and patterns in the room; consider plaid, check, or narrow stripe. Use a durable, washable cotton fabric and a simple twill tape or grosgrain ribbon for the trim.

MATERIALS

- Framed freestanding shelving unit
- Fabric (for measuring tips, see pages 179–81)
- Trimming tape, 2.5cm (1in) wide
- Circular template for scallops, such as a plate, saucer, or cup, ¼ the width of the cupboard, or a compass and paper to make a pattern
- Sewing kit (see pages 170–3)

Simple fabric ties provide a finishing flourish on this fabric-covered set of shelves, which can be used to conceal a variety of items, such as toys or clothes.

1 For the cupboard back, measure the height (A) and width (B) of the frame and add 2.5cm (1in) to both measurements for the seam allowance. Measure, mark, and cut one panel to these dimensions. For the sides and front, measure the depth of the frame (C), add half the width (B) and again add 2.5cm (1in). Measure, mark and cut two pieces of fabric to this dimension by the height (A) plus 2.5cm (1in) – make sure to match patterns with the back panel.

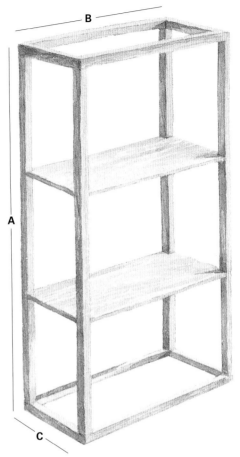

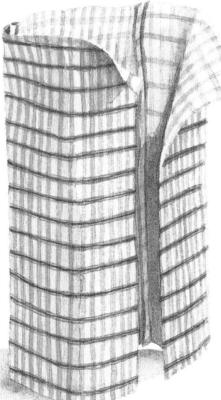

2 With right sides facing and raw edges matching, pin and sew the back panel to the side/front panels with 1.25cm (½in) seams.

3 Fold and press the front and bottom edges 1.25cm (½in) towards the right side of the fabric. Pin trimming tape over the folded edge all around, turning ends under by 1.25cm (½in) and folding to mitre the corners (see page 176). Topstitch in place to hide the raw edges.

4 Measure the depth (C) and width (B) of the top of the frame adding 2.5cm (1in) to each dimension. Measure, mark, and cut a top panel to these dimensions. With right sides facing and raw edges matching, pin the top panel to the side/front and back panels, centering the trimmed front edges in the middle of one long side. Sew the panels together with a 1.25cm (½in) seam. Place the cover over the frame to check the fit.

5 To make the scalloped border, divide the frame width (B) by four – the diameter of your circular template should equal this figure (or use a compass to draw a template). Ideally, the frame depth (C) will be twice the diameter of the template. If not, you will need to adjust the fit at the back (see step 8).

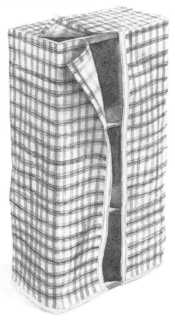

6 The length of your border is B + B + C + C plus 2.5cm (1in). For the width of the border, double the diameter of your template and add 2.5cm (1in). Measure, mark, and cut fabric to these dimensions. Fold the fabric in half lengthwise, right sides facing, press. Measure and mark the centre of the border crosswise, and centre your template over this point, leaving 1.25cm (½in) extending at the raw edge side. Trace halfway around the template to form the centre scallop. Continue tracing the template along the border to the ends.

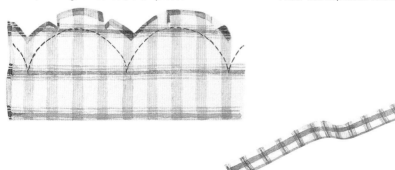

7 Machine-stitch along the drawn lines. Cut out scallops 6mm (¼in) outside these lines. Clip the curves, turn right side out, then press.

8 Centre the middle scallop over the centre front of the top of the unit, and pin the border in place. Hand-sew the border to the top, using a hemming stitch (see page 174). Fold in the raw edges of the back centre scallop by 1.25cm (½in) and slipstitch closed.

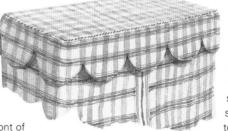

9 To make the ties, measure, mark, and cut four 50 by 10cm (20 by 4in) strips of fabric. Right sides facing, fold and press each strip lengthwise. Machine-stitch the long edges together with 6mm (¼in) seams. Stitch one short end of each strip at a 45 degree angle; trim off the excess fabric. Turn right side out and press. Fold in the raw edges of each strip 6mm (¼in) and press flat. Pin the ties to the cover in pairs, 30cm (12in) and 60cm (24in) from the top, and 2.5cm (1in) from each edge. To attach the ties, machine-stitch a square shape at the end of the tie, closing the open ends at the same time, or hand-sew them in place.

Sunflower Appliqué Chair Cover

A cover of white cotton canvas with sunny yellow accents, gives this plain wooden dining chair a dressed up appearance for a summer gathering. Partial slits at the corners of the full-length skirt avoid the need for zips or other closures and make the loose cover easy to slip on and off for cleaning and storage. Piping around the edges keeps the look crisp, and a bright sunflower appliqué – cut out from contrasting fabric and sewn to the back – adds a personal touch. Why not create two or three sets of covers for other seasons? Try a lighter-weight sateen or chintz for spring or a heavier-weight velveteen for autumn and winter.

MATERIALS

- Armless chair
- Main fabric (for measuring tips, see pages 178–81)
- Contrasting fabric for piping and appliqué
- Piping cord
- Fusible webbing or fabric stiffener
- Sewing kit (see pages 170–3)

By careful use of bright colours for their dining chair covers, the owners of this house have linked the indoor living area to the outdoor space.

1 Measure the chair back from the top to the floor, following any curves in the chair (A), and the width of the back along the top (B). Add 2.5cm (1in) to both these dimensions. Measure, mark, and cut a piece of fabric to these dimensions for the back panel.

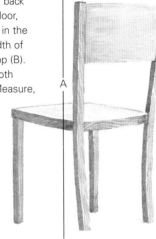

2 Measure the front of the chair from the top of the back rest to the back of the seat and from the back of the seat to the front of the seat (C). Measure across the front of the seat (D) and note whether this dimension equals or is different from (B). Add 2.5cm (1in) to each dimension for seam allowances. Using (C) as the length and (B) and (D) as the width measurements, measure, mark and cut a piece of fabric to these dimensions. Note: If (B) and (D) are different, centre them at either end of the length measurement. The length cutting lines will need to be drawn at a slant to join with the width lines at each end. Once the length measurement is determined and width lines are centred and marked, mark the slanted sides.

3 Measure the chair seat height from the top of the seat to the floor (E). For the front of the skirt, measure, mark and cut a piece of fabric, using (E) and (D) as length and width dimensions and adding 2.5cm (1in) to each measurement for seam allowances. Measure the side of the seat from the back of the back leg to the front of the seat (F). For the sides of the skirt, measure, mark and cut two pieces of fabric, using (E) and (F) as the length and width dimensions and adding 2.5cm (1in) to each measurement for seam allowances.

4 Make enough corded piping to edge the hems of the skirt and every seam of the entire loose cover (see pages 176–7).

5 Iron the contrasting fabric appliqué to the fusible webbing or fabric stiffener. Cut out the shape.

6 Pin the appliqué to the centre of the top half of the right side of the back panel and machine- or hand-sew the appliqué to the back panel using satin stitch (see page 174).

7 With right sides facing and raw edges matching, pin and tack the corded piping to the front panel. Using a zipper foot, machine-sew the piping in place with a 1.25cm (½in) seam. Trim the excess cord, fold under the fabric covering, and hand-sew to finish the piping ends.

8 On the seam allowance of the front panel, mark the points where the seat meets the backrest. With right sides facing, raw edges matching, pin and tack the top of the back panel to the top of the front panel, sandwiching the piping between the panels. Using a zipper foot, machine-sew the front panel to the back panel with a 1.25cm (½in) seam up to the marks. Clip into the seam allowance at the marks.

9 With right sides facing and raw edges matching, pin and tack the bottom of the front panel to the tops of the skirt front and side panels, sandwiching piping between panels. Using a zipper foot, machine-sew the front panel to the skirt panels with a 1.25cm (½in) seam. Join the top portion of the skirt panels by machine-sewing 1.25cm (½in) seams from the seat down ⅓ the length of the skirt, leaving the bottoms free to trim with piping.

10 With right sides facing and raw edges matching, pin and tack the corded piping around the skirt slits and hem all around. Using a zipper foot, machine-sew the piping in place with a 1.25cm (½in) seam. Trim cord, fold under the fabric covering, and hand-sew to finish the piping ends. Trim and finish the raw edges of the seam allowance with machine zigzag or overlock stitch, or overlock by hand (see page 175), if desired. Press, and slip the cover over the chair.

Pleated Tablecloth

For special occasions a well-dressed table is a must. And this crisp, pleated tablecloth, here made from fine-printed Fortuny-style fabric, adds a touch of formality without being stuffy. Its clean, made-to-measure tailored lines keep the look modern, while dressmaker details, such as corded frog closures at the tops of the box pleats, elevate the elegance quotient. A damask would work equally well, or a use crisp linen or calendered (glazed) solid cotton fabric with tab closures as a variation for a minimalist setting; a floral print with bows in a contrasting fabric would create a more romantic effect.

MATERIALS
- Fabric* (for measuring tips, see pages 179–81)
- Six frog fasteners
- Glass-headed pins
- Sewing kit (see pages 170–3)

* The instructions are given for a 72.5cm (29 in) high table, measuring 1.5m x 1m (5ft x 3ft). Adjust number of fabric widths per side as needed, depending on your table size and fabric width.

The neat box pleats of the tablecloth harmonize with the sharp-edged covers used for the chairs, adding elegance to this contemporary dining set.

1 Measure the length and width of the table top and add 2.5cm (1in) to each dimension. Measure, mark, and cut a piece of fabric for the top of the tablecloth to these dimensions, centring the fabric pattern.

2 For the skirt, measure, mark, and cut six widths of fabric, making each 7.5cm (3in) deeper than the height of your table. Make sure that the same pattern appears on all the widths before cutting.

3 To make the skirt panels for one long side, join the short edges of one side of two of the widths, right sides facing and raw edges matching, with a 1.25cm (½in) seam. Repeat for the other long side. Press open the seams.

4 To make the box pleat, place one pair of joined panels, right side up, on a work surface. With the seam in the centre, fold a double pleat, 10cm (4in) wide, to the left and to the right of the seam. (The back of the fully folded double pleat should measure 20cm/8in across.) Pin in place and press.

5 To secure each box pleat, place the joined panels on a work surface. Remove the pins, fold the panels in half along the seam line, right sides facing, and stretch the folded pleat out flat. Machine-stitch from the top of the panel about 7.5cm (3in) down the set of creased pleat lines furthest from the seam. Refold the pleats and secure them by tacking 6mm (¼in) along the top allowance.

6 Place the entire side panel on a work surface, right side up. Measure points 75cm (30in) on either side of the centre line of the box pleat and use pins to mark them.

8 Pleat the short panels of the tablecloth. Place one of the remaining cut widths on a work surface, right side up. Fold in half, selvages aligned, to find the centre. Measure and use pins to mark points 45cm (18in) to either side of the centre line. The total distance between pins should equal the width of the table. Repeat for the other short panel.

9 As in step 7, starting at a point marked by a pin, fold in and press a double pleat, 10cm (4in) wide, at each end of the panel. Add an extra 1.25cm (½in) on the second pleats for seam allowance. Cut off any excess fabric. Repeat for the last panel.

10 Place one short side panel over one long side panel, right sides facing and raw edges matching; pin. Join the panels with a 1.25cm (½in) seam.

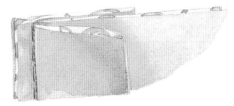

7 Make another pleat, 10cm (4in) wide, at each end of the panel. First, with wrong sides facing, fold and press a crease down the panel at the pin mark. Then measure another point 10cm (4in) from the first fold and mark it with a pin. With right sides facing, make and press a fold, 11.25cm (4½in) wide, at this point. (The extra 1.25cm/½in is the seam allowance to join the panels with the short sides of the tablecloth.) Repeat at the other end of the panel. Cut off any excess fabric. Repeat steps 4–7 for the other long panel; set both panels aside.

11 To secure the corner pleat, repeat the process described in step 5. Repeat steps 10 and 11 until all four sides are joined to form the skirt.

12 Turn the skirt wrong side out and, starting at one corner and using pins, attach the tablecloth top to the skirt. Tack the two pieces together, then machine-stitch with a 1.25cm (½in) seam allowance. Finish the seams by machine-stitching with zigzag or overlock stitch, or overlock by hand (see page 175).

13 To finish the skirt, fold and press a 3.25cm (1½in) double hem along the bottom. Machine-sew with hem stitch and a blind hem foot (see page 178), or hand-sew with hemming stitch (see page 174). Hand-sew the frog fasteners at the top of each pleat about 2.5cm (1in) below the tabletop.

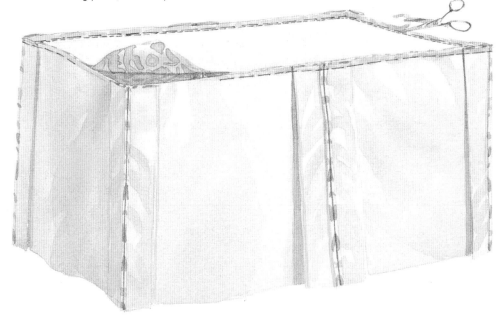

Occasional Chair Cover

Topped with this pretty loose cover, any plain occasional chair will be at home among finer upholstered furnishings in a living room or sitting area. The best foundation for a loose cover like this is a straight-back chair with a padded seat. Make the loose cover from cotton canvas (as here) or linen fabric in a creamy neutral colour as this will enable you to move the chair unobtrusively from room to room in the house, sidling it up to a desk in a home office or providing extra seating in a living room or sunroom when you have company. The loose cover is easy to remove for washing, or perhaps so that you can ring the changes with another cover in a different colour.

MATERIALS
- Upright wooden chair
- Fabric (for measuring tips, see pages 179–81)
- Sewing kit (see page 170–3)

A shallow gusset around the seat edge gives this loose cover some structure, while the ruffled skirt and tie closures add old-world charm.

1 For the front of the cover, measure the front of the chair from the top of the back rest to the back of the seat and from the back of the seat to the front of the seat (A). Measure across the top of the chair back (B). Measure across the front of the seat (C) and note whether this dimension equals or is different from (B). Add 5cm (2in) to each dimension. Using (A) as the length measurement and (B) and (C) as the width measurements, measure, mark, and cut a piece of fabric to these dimensions. If (B) and (C) are different, centre them at either end of the length measurement. The length cutting lines will need to be drawn at a slant to join with the width lines at each end. Once the length measurement is determined and the width lines are centred at either end of it and marked, mark the slanted sides.

2 Measure the height of the chair back from the top of the back rest to the bottom of the seat base (D). For the back of the cover, measure, mark, and cut a piece of fabric, using (D) and (B) as length and width dimensions respectively and adding 5cm (2in) to each measurement for seam allowances.

3 For the seat gusset, measure from the back of the seat to the front of the seat. Double this measurement and add the width of the seat front (C) plus 10cm (4in). Measure, mark, and cut a strip of fabric to this length by 10cm (4in) wide.

4 For the front ruffle, multiply the gusset length by 1½. Measure, mark, and cut a piece of fabric to this length by 20cm (8in) wide. For the back ruffle, add 5cm (2in) to the chair back width (B) and multiply by 1½. Measure, mark, and cut a piece of fabric to this length by 20cm (8in) wide.

5 Place the front panel, right side up, on a work surface. With right sides facing and raw edges matching, pin and tack the front gusset along the seat front and sides of the front panel; centre the gusset over the seat front then wrap it around the sides. Machine-stitch the gusset to the front panel with a 1.25cm (½in) seam. Cut small notches at the front corners to allow the fabric to lie flat.

6 Place the back panel, right side up, on a work surface. With right sides facing and raw edges matching, place the front panel over the back panel and pin the top and sides together. Slip the cover over the chair to ensure a neat but loose fit. Cut two small notches on the side seam allowances, 10cm (4in) from the bottom of the back to mark the openings.

7 Remove the pinned cover from the chair and machine-stitch the back to the front from notch to notch with a 1.25cm (½in) seam.

8 Fold and press a 1.25cm (½in) double hem along the bottom and sides of both pieces of ruffle fabric.

9 Hand-sew a row of running stitches (see page 173) 6mm (¼in) from the top raw edge of both pieces of ruffle fabric. Pull the tails of the thread to create the ruffling, until the longer fabric strip is exactly the length of the front and sides of the seat and the shorter fabric strip is exactly the length of the back of the seat.

10 With right sides facing and raw edges matching, pin and tack the longer ruffle to the front and sides of the gusset. Machine-sew with a 1.25cm (½in) seam. Repeat for the back ruffle, pinning, tacking, and machine-stitching to the back panel with a 1.25cm (½in) seam.

11 To make the ties, measure, mark, and cut 4 strips of fabric 50cm (20in) long by 3.75cm (1½in) wide. Fold and press in the sides by 6mm (¼in) all around, mitring the corners (see page 176).

12 Fold and press each strip in half lengthwise, wrong sides facing. Topstitch close to the edges all around.

13 Finish the raw edges of the openings at the back of the chair cover by folding under and pressing 6mm (¼in) double hems and machine- or hand-sewing with hemming stitch (see page 174). Machine- or hand-sew the ties to the front and back of the openings along the skirt seam allowance.

Fitted Wingchair Cover

Made in a fresh-looking fabric, this fitted loose cover spruces up an old wingchair – so long as it has good bones and its springs haven't sprung or its seat hasn't sagged. If you prefer a classic look, make the cover from traditional *toile de Jouy* or choose a linen in a solid neutral colour. Alternatively, rejuvenate the chair by painting the legs black, white, or red, and creating the cover from a graphic print or bright solid colour and trimming it with contrasting piping. Meticulous measuring and attention to detail when fitting and matching patterns before sewing are the keys to success with this cover.

MATERIALS

- Fabric (for measuring tips, see page 179–81)
- Contrasting fabric for piping
- Piping cord
- T-pins
- Glass-headed pins
- Cotton binding tape
- Sewing kit (see pages 170–3)

A fitted loose cover with contrasting piping and tie closures revitalizes an antique wingchair.

1 Measure the height and width of the front of the chair back and add 10cm (4in) to both dimensions. Making sure the grain is straight and the pattern is centred and square, measure, mark, and cut a piece of fabric to these dimensions. Using T-pins, pin the panel to the chair, right side facing out and pattern centred. Start pinning at the centres of the top and bottom, then the middle of the sides, to create quadrants. Smooth out the fabric towards the edges as you go. Continue pinning and smoothing fabric between the first four pins until the panel is tautly pinned all around. Trim the edges of the fabric, leaving a 1.25cm (½in) seam allowance around the top and sides and 10cm (4in) along the bottom for tucking in where the back meets the seat.

2 Remove the pins and take the fabric panel off the chair. Along the bottom edge of the panel, cut three 8.25cm (3¼in) long vertical slits – one in the centre and the other two 5cm (2in) from the centre slit. Then measure, mark, and cut three triangular pieces of fabric, measuring 8.75cm (3½in) along two sides and 3.75cm (1½in) along the bottom.

3 With right sides facing down, fold in and press the edges of each triangle by 6mm (¼in) all around.

4 With right sides facing up, pin a triangle over each slit of the chair back panel and topstitch in place. Replace the panel, right side up, on the front of the chair back, and pin in place again using T-pins.

5 For the inside of the arms, measure the width and depth of the chair arms, from the back of the seat all the way around the front of the arm to the side seam of the arm, and from the side seam at the top of the arm to the seat. Add 10cm (4in) to both measurements. Making sure the grain is straight and the pattern is centred and square, measure, mark, and cut two pieces of fabric to these dimensions. Using T-pins, pin each panel to the arms of the chair, right side facing out and pattern centred as in step 1. At the top front of each arm, fold in a dart to make the fabric fit the chair arm. (To finish the dart see step 16, page 160). When the fabric is fully pinned in place, trim the edges, leaving a 1.25cm (½in) seam allowance around the top and sides and 10cm (4in) along the bottom for tucking in where the arms sides meet the seat. Leave all the panels pinned in place.

6 For the seat, measure the depth and width of the chair seat at the widest part and add 10cm (4in) to both measurements. Making sure the grain is straight and the pattern centred and square, measure, mark, and cut a piece of fabric to these dimensions. Using T-pins, pin the panel to the seat of the chair, right side facing out and pattern centred as in step 1. When fabric is fully pinned in place, trim the edges, leaving a 1.25cm (½in) seam allowance along the front edge and 10cm (4in) around the sides and back for tucking in. For the back edge of the seat, cut and fit triangles as in steps 2–4, then replace the panel, pinning it in place again.

8 For the chair back and outside of the arms, measure the height of the back; now measure its width, from the seam on the outside front of the arm to the midpoint of the back of the chair. Add 15cm (6in) to both measurements. Making sure the grain is vertical and straight and the pattern is square, measure, mark, and cut two pieces of fabric to these dimensions. Using T-pins, pin one panel to the outside arm and back of the chair, right side facing out and pattern centred as in step 1. When the fabric is fully pinned in place, trim the edges, leaving a 1.25cm (½in) seam allowance along the curved top and side edges; leave 10cm (4in) along the centre of the back for overlap, and 7.5cm (3in) along the bottom for turning under. Along the vertical edge of the 10cm (4in) overlap, fold in and pin a 2.5cm (1in). Leave the panel pinned in place.

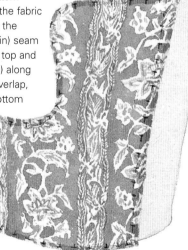

7 For the chair seat front, measure the depth and width of the area below the front of the chair seat from outside seam to outside seam and add 10cm (4in) to both measurements. Making sure the grain is vertical and straight and the pattern is centred and square, measure, mark, and cut a piece of fabric to these dimensions. Using T-pins, pin the panel to the seat and bottom of the chair arms, right side facing out and pattern centred as in step 1. When the fabric is fully pinned in place, trim the edges, leaving a 1.25cm (½in) seam allowance along the top and side edges and 7.5cm (3in) along the bottom for turning under. Leave the panel pinned in place.

9 Using T-pins, pin the other half of the outside back and arm panel to the chair, right side facing out, matching the pattern to the opposite side and aligning the pattern along the centre at the back. When the fabric is fully pinned in place, trim the edges, leaving a 1.25cm (½in) seam allowance along the curved top and side edges, 10cm (4in) along the centre of the back for overlap, and 7.5cm (3in) along the bottom for turning under. Along the vertical edge of the 10cm (4in) overlap, fold in and pin a 3.75cm (1½in) double fold. Leave the panel pinned in place.

10 With all panels pinned in place, use your fingers to pull up and align the raw edges of the seam allowance, wrong sides facing, all around and use glass-headed pins to mark the line of the seam. When all pins are in place and the cover fits perfectly, mark the seam lines on the wrong side of the fabric by pressing open the seam allowance and marking the creases with tailor's chalk. Leaving the pins in place, cut notches through the raw edges of both layers of the seam allowance all around the chair at roughly 10cm (4in) intervals.

11 Remove the T-pins. And remove the cover from the chair, leaving the glass-headed pins in place. The glass-headed pins, the chalk-marked seam lines, and the notches will serve as the seam guides for the panels.

12 With cover removed, gradually work around the pins to invert the seam lines so they are on the wrong side of the fabric. Do this by removing the pins one by one, carefully inverting the seam allowance, and re-pinning in place on the wrong side of the fabric. Continue in this manner, aligning notches, until entire cover is turned wrong side out and ready for seaming.

13 Tack along all the pinned seam lines, except the seam that runs across the front of the seat and the long, shaped seam that curves from the legs along the sides, top of the arms, and top of the chair. (These two seams will be finished with corded piping.) Machine-stitch all other panels with 1.25cm (½ in) seams.

14 Measure the unfinished seams and make up enough piping (see pages 176–7) to run along them. With raw edges matching and right sides facing, sandwich the piping between the seam allowance of the shaped edges of the chair and along the chair front between the two arms, re-pinning in place. Tack. Cut further small snips along curved edges and corners so the fabric lies flat and fits neatly.

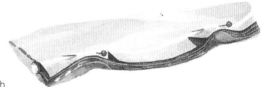

15 Using a zipper foot, machine-stitch piping between the seam allowances with a 1.25cm (½in) seam.

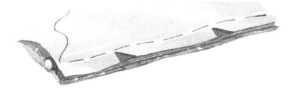

16 On the wrong side of the fabric, hand-stitch along the dart line pinned in step 5 using a running stitch or slip stitch (see page 173).

17 Turn the whole cover right side out and press. Machine- or hand-sew the vertical double hems of both back panels with hemming stitch (see page 174). Fold in and press a 6mm (¼in) double hem around the bottom edge of the cover. Machine-topstitch in place. Slip the cover over the chair and tuck in the flaps at the sides and back of the seat.

18 Along both sides of each leg, snip vertical cuts into the fabric up to 6mm (¼in) from the bottom edge of the chair, so that the fabric lies flat on all sides. Finish the edges of each incision with zigzag stitch or overlock stitch by machine or overlock by hand. Fold up the hems around the chair corners at each leg and finger-press in place.

19 Turn the chair on its back, fold in the bottom flaps, and fold and pin a series of 7.5cm (3in) darts around the curves of the back so the flap lies flat. Remove the cover from the chair.

20 Hand-sew the darts and then hem the chair corner flaps to the cover by hand, keeping the finger-pressed creases in place.

21 Cut 13 pieces of binding tape, each 3.75cm (1½in) long. Fold each piece in half and, following the positions indicated in the illustration for step 19, hand-sew the loops to the bottom edge of the cover. Place the cover back on the chair.

22 Turn the chair on its back. Cut a very long piece of binding tape and thread the tape through the loops in a crossover pattern as indicated in the illustration for step 19 and tie the ends in a bow. Pulling under the bottom edge in this manner will give the cover a crisp fitted appearance.

23 To make the closure ties at the back of the cover, measure, mark, and cut ten strips of contrasting fabric, 30cm (12in) long by 6.25cm (2½in) wide. Fold each strip in half lengthwise, right sides facing. Machine-sew along the long side and one short side. With the blunt end of a pencil, turn each strip right side out. Tuck in the raw edges of the remaining short end and press. Slipstitch to close neatly.

24 Starting with ties at the bottom edge, measure and mark the placement of the ties at regular intervals along both sides of the back centre opening. Hand-sew the ties in place, or remove the cover and machine-sew. Tie the pairs of ties into a bow.

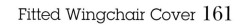

fabrics & techniques

Whether you plan to make country-style café curtains or formal draperies, casual floor cushions or luxurious bolsters, the fabric you choose will play a leading role in the overall impact of your creations. Colour and pattern are the most obvious characteristics of a fabric. But these are only part of the design equation. A fabric's fibre content, weave, weight, opacity, and finish also need to be considered when making your choice. In addition, understanding its performance characteristics will help you select a fabric that is suitable for its intended purpose and will yield the best results.

fabrics

Fabric Composition

Historically, curtains were made from natural fabrics – wool, linen, silk, and cotton, and these fabrics continue to remain popular today. In the past synthetic fabrics were not very popular but advances in technology have resulted in synthetics that look and feel almost like natural fabrics. They are also stronger and less likely to fade than fabrics made of natural fibres. Many fabrics also include a mix of natural and synthetic fibres to improve durability, while offering the drape and feel of natural fibres. Since the qualities of the fibres affect performance of the finished fabric, those qualities should be considered in choosing the appropriate fabric for your requirements.

Synthetic Fibres

Acetates: Fabrics made of acetate hang well, are fairly resistant to deterioration and sun damage, but they can burn quickly unless they are treated with fire retardants. They should be dry-cleaned.

Acrylic: Although fabrics made with acrylic fibres drape well, they can stretch. They are very resistant to deterioration, soiling, and light, but melt or burn under fire. They can be machine-washed, but creases must be pressed out with steam.

Modacrylic: These fabrics hang well – although they may stretch – and are very good at resisting deterioration and sun fading. They are flame-resistant and are washable.

Nylon: Nylon fabrics build up static, but are fairly resistant to deterioration. They are very resistant to sun fading and are washable, but they will melt in a fire and need to be treated to reduce this risk.

Polyesters: These fabrics are crease-resistant, but may stretch. They don't suffer from deterioration or sun damage and are machine washable. They are flammable unless treated.

Rayon: Rayons hang well, but tend to stretch, are fairly resistant to deterioration and sun damage, but burn like paper unless they are specially treated. Some are washable; others require dry-cleaning. Always check the label.

Natural Fibres

Cotton: Cotton fabrics drape well, resist deterioration, and are quite resistant to fading by the sun. They are highly flammable unless treated.

Linens: Fabrics made with linen fibres hang well, but crease easily. They are durable and resistant to sun damage, but have a high burning rate unless treated. They must be dry-cleaned. Creases must be pressed out with steam.

Silk: While they can be beautiful and lustrous and they hang well, silk fabrics are fragile and are easily damaged by sunlight. They burn rapidly if ignited and should be dry-cleaned.

Wool: Wool fabrics hang well, are durable, and are resistant to sun damage, but they are prone to damage by moths. They need to be dry-cleaned. Naturally flame retardant, wool burns slowly and may self-extinguish.

Common Weaves

Along with the different fibres and yarns, the weave of a fabric can vary. The type of loom along with the type of fibre, determines fabric weight and construction characteristics. The yarns or threads of a fabric are organized as warp yarns, which run the vertical or lengthwise grain of the fabric, and weft yarns, which run horizontally across the grain. Warp yarns carry the weight of the fabric, weft yarns are the filling yarns of a fabric.

Basket weave: Two or more warp yarns crossing two or more weft yarns in a consistent fashion resembling a woven basket.

Dobby weave: A decorative weave with small designs or patterns woven into the fabric structure.

Jacquard weave: Any fabric woven on a Jacquard loom, often with complex patterning.

Leno weave: A fabric with warp yarns organized in pairs, one yarn is twisted around the other between picks of the weft yarns.

Pile weaves: Fabric woven with a looped pile that is either cut, as in velvet or velveteen, or uncut, as in terry cloth.

Plain weave: The simplest of weaves with each weft thread crossing over one warp thread, then under the next and so on.

Rib weave: A plain weave with heavy threads either in the warp direction or the weft direction.

Satin weave: A weave in which the face of the fabric consists of only warp or weft threads, giving the surface a smooth finish.

Twill weave: Similar to a plain weave except that warp yarns skip at predetermined intervals to create diagonal ribs in the weave.

Colour and Pattern

Colour matching is important. Always measure carefully so that you buy enough fabric for your project at the outset (see pages 179–81). If you have to buy more, you may well find that the new fabric comes from a different dye batch, so the colours will vary slightly from your first purchase. Fabrics are coloured or printed using a variety of dyeing or printing methods, each of which produce different effects.

Dyeing Methods

The raw woven fabrics are known as greige (pronounced grey) goods. Some greige goods may be piece dyed, where finished lengths of cloth are dyed. Other processes involve dyeing in the fibre stage, for example, stock dyeing or fibre dyeing, when the basic fibres are dyed before they're spun into yarn. Some synthetic fibres are coloured with a process called solution dyeing. The dyes or pigments are added to the viscose from which the fibre forms are extruded. The resulting fibres are completely saturated with colour and very fade-resistant. In another method, yarn dyeing, the yarns are dyed before they're woven into fabric.

There are also numerous ways to colour a fabric by printing. Fabrics can be hand-printed, including block printing, silk screening, stencilling, and hand painting, which results in beautiful designs with a hand-rendered appearance.

There are also semi-automated and rotary-printing methods that use screens to apply colours and patterns in layers to the face of the fabric. With roller printing, specially engraved rollers press the colour and pattern onto the fabric. These methods result in very uniform designs.

Working with Patterns

Patterns can be printed onto a fabric or woven into it, as on a jacquard or dobby loom. Some fabrics also incorporate patterns made by both methods.

When choosing a patterned fabric, it is important to be mindful of the size of the repeat when calculating how much fabric you need. The repeat is the size of the basic design, from top to bottom and side to side. Most standard repeats are multiples, either up or down, of 33.75cm (13½in). When matching a pattern, note that they begin and end at the selvage line and are usually cut in half. Understanding the type of repeat on any given patterned fabric enables you to match the repeats properly and buy enough fabric at the outset.

It is also important to choose a fabric with a pattern repeat that is appropriate to the scale of

your project. Small patterns such as tiny all-over motifs can produce the effect of texture, rather than pattern, and can be used to link other colours in a room. Large patterns will command attention and dominate the room. They can also make a space look smaller.

The direction of the pattern is also an important consideration. Most patterns, including stripes, checks, tartans, and other motifs, run parallel to the length of the fabric and must be precisely matched. Others patterns are non-directional. This includes all-over patterns, and patterns that appear to be random, with motifs in an unbalanced composition. Although they appear as random, these patterns *will* have a horizontal repeat that must be matched. In some situations, you may want to turn a directional pattern, such as a stripe, on its side to reorient the direction from up and down to side to side to cover a wide area. This process, known as "railroading", can make pattern-matching difficult.

Some patterns feature primary and secondary repeats, which require you to make a choice about which you want to highlight, others are print-on-print repeats, such as a woven jacquard fabric topped with a printed pattern. With these fabrics, both repeats need to be matched.

Balanced patterns are those in which the whole repeat is balanced on both selvage edges. Here

the seams run through secondary motifs. Halved patterns, on the other hand, are cut in half at the selvage edges – for these the seam will run through the centre of the motif when joining cut widths (see pages 179–81).

With half drop or drop match patterns, the patterns shift on the diagonal so that the pattern on one selvage edge with not match the pattern on the other, so additional fabric will be required to match patterns. Straight repeat patterns have motifs that run across the width of the fabric and patterns will match on both sides of the selvage.

Fabric Finishes

Standard and decorative finish treatments can be applied to a textile to add its durability, enhance its performance, and/or affect its surface qualities, for example flammability. Some may be added by the manufacturer and others you can apply yourself. Check the labels of fabrics when you buy them.

Standard Fabric Finishes

Antibacterial: Suppresses mould and mildew.
Care: Enhances ease of care of a fabric by resisting wrinkles.
Flame retardant: Slows the rate of ignition and burning and, in some situations, enables a fabric to extinguish flames.
Insulating: Insulates a fabric from light, sound, or temperature via a backing, usually foam.
Laminating: Reinforces fabric with a laminated knitted backing.
Mothproofing: Protects from insect infestation.
Soil-repellent: Shrugs off surface dirt and stains.
Water-repellent: Used on outdoor fabrics to make them less water absorbent.

Decorative Finishes

Brightening: Enhances a fabric's colours so that they last longer.
Calendering: Polishes the surface with starches, glazes, or resins pressed into the fabric with a heavy roller.

Chintz: Glazed to add shine to the fabric.

De-lustring: Removes a shiny finish from a fabric.

Embossing: Uses an engraved roller to press a permanent design into the fabric.

Etching or burn-out: An acid wash that burns out or etches a design into a sheer fabric.

Flocking: Bonds small fibres to the surface to produce a raised pattern.

Moiré: Embosses fabric with a watermark pattern.

Napping: Brushes fibres to create a short pile or fuzzy soft surface.

Panne: Embosses velvets or velours in one direction to create a pattern.

Plissé: Uses acid to pucker the yarns of fabric.

Other Finishes

You can also buy spray-on finishing products, such as *Scotchgard* or *Ultra-Guard*, that resist stains, water, and other forms of damage. Always read the manufacturer's instructions before applying these and test them on a fabric scrap before use as some will affect the colour.

Matching Finish to Project

Be sure to choose a fabric with appropriate finish characteristics for your project. For curtains, heavy-weight fabrics, such as velvet, won't hold fullness to the degree a lighter-weight fabric will, nor will they gather as well or be as easy to pleat unless the pleats are very deep.

Velvet is also difficult for making loose covers for furniture, as some of the seams will have several layers of fabric and the nap can cause the layers to slip. Unless you're very experienced, use velvets and other heavily napped fabrics for simpler projects, such as cushions. You will require larger quantities of lighter-weight fabrics to get the fullness you may desire for curtains.

Certain fragile fabrics, such as silk, and loosely woven fabrics are not also good choices for loose covers, as they won't withstand wear and tear. In addition, avoid using upholstery-weight fabrics, especially those with latex or adhesive backings,

for loose covers or curtains. Instead choose medium-weight tightly woven fabrics, such as plain weaves, rib weaves, twills, and canvases. Be aware that geometric patterns are tricky to match around chair arms. Avoid slippery fabrics with a sheen for any loose cover that needs to be tucked into a chair's decking. Also, avoid using dress-making fabrics; they simply don't stand up to the wear. Home decorating fabrics are specially manufactured for durability and must pass standard rub and abrasion tests.

Fabric Widths

The majority of home decorating fabrics are 137cm (54in) wide, but there are exceptions. Quilting cottons are typically 114cm (45in), as are some high-end silks and linens. Knit fabrics can come in 152cm (60in), and sheers come in several widths – 137cm (54in), 152cm (60in), and 270cm (106in). Extra-wide curtain sheers can be 274–320cm (108–126in) wide and extra-wide jacquards can range from 289–290cm (114–116in). Curtain lining material is available in virtually every width, from 120–320cm (48–126in).

Remember that the bolt width of the fabric includes the selvage edges, while the usable width of fabric measures from one selvage allowance to the other. Selvage allowances can vary too. Take this into account when making your calculation.

Where a fabric is not wide enough for one width to cover a project, whole widths can be joined for curtains (see page 180), but for objects where the joining seam will be visible, it is better to position the whole width centrally on the item and cut pieces to go on either side of it to make up the width – this means you will end up with two seams, but they will be symmetrical on the item.

Lining, Backing, and Padding

With the exception of sheers, all curtain fabrics are enhanced when backed with a fixed or detachable lining. Lining not only adds body, but it also improves the way the curtains hang. In addition

lining can block out unwanted sunlight, buffer noise, protect your floors, carpets, furnishings, and curtain fabrics from dirt, moisture, and fading.

Several different types of fabric are used to line curtains, but cotton sateen is the most common. This is a tightly woven, slightly polished fabric that doesn't absorb dirt and dust. It is available in varying widths and colours, white and ivory being the most common.

Newer sateen linings, which are shiny on one side and napped on the other, further enhance the way a curtain hangs and provide an extra layer of thermal insulation – blocking heat out in summer and insulating from cold in winter.

There are linings that are specifically designed to control heat and cold. Aluminium-coated lining material reflects sunlight but if you're considering this type of lining, bear in mind its effect on your neighbours. Thermal suede has a rubber backing for insulation. Some lining materials double up and provide thermal insulation and reduce, or completely black out, light too.

Black-out linings provide maximum light blocking capability. To prevent needle holes that can permit light to pass through, consider glue-tacking the widths together before you sew them. French or black lining can be used to line or interline (see below) and provide a black-out effect or prevent colour bleed-through, but they can also make the face-side of the fabric look grey.

Fixed linings are sewn directly into the curtain, while detachable linings are secured with special lining tape. When choosing a lining, opt for one that closely matches the fibre, colour, and weight of the decorative fabric. And be mindful of the extra weight that linings will add to the overall treatment so that you can be sure your curtain track and fixings will support them.

Interlinings

Fragile fabrics, such as silk, should not be used to make curtains unless they are protected by an interlining. This is an extra lining that is fixed

between the lining and the face fabric. Made with a non-woven construction, interlinings also add bulk and thermal control not only to curtains but also to quilts and bedcovers. They come in several weights, widths, and thicknesses, and if you need to join several widths together for wide panels, overlap the edges and join them with herringbone stitch (see page 174). The thickest type of interlining is known as bump and resembles a fleecy blanket. Other options include domett, which is a coarse flannel, baize (felt), or thinner bonded synthetic interlinings, which are good to use with synthetic or lightweight fabrics.

Buckram and other fabric stiffeners can be sewn into curtain headings or ironed onto the back of a pelmet to strengthen it and provide a smooth crisp surface. Pellon is another stiffener that is softer than buckram and almost seems as if it isn't there. Peel-away stabilizers are useful if you are embroidering monograms and other motifs.

Padding: When you're creating soft furnishings that are padded, foam padding or wadding will provide a layer of softness or bulk. These are available in a variety of thicknesses and sizes and made from natural or synthetic fibres. Padding can be used to soften fabric-covered wooden pelmets, lambrequins, or headboards. They are also great for puffing up chair cushions, adding bulk to the hems of tablecloths, or when sandwiched between the fabric layers of a quilt. Like interlining, if such padding has to be joined, the edge of one sheet should overlap the other and be sewn together with herringbone stitch (see p.174).

Cleaning and Care

Part of the appeal of any fabric loose cover is the fact that it can be easily removed for cleaning. However, although many fabrics can be machine-washed and dried, most decorator fabrics are treated with a finish or sizing, which may resist stains, keep the fabric crisp, provide lustre, or protect the fabric from fading. All of these fabrics should be dry-cleaned. The same holds true for curtains and blinds. Even if your fabric claims to be machine-washable, repeated washing can stress the seams as well as the fabric fibres. Dry-cleaning is the best way to clean them to preserve the integrity of the fabric as well as its construction. The one exception is polyester fabric, which can be hand-washed in a bath.

It sounds obvious, but, if you plan to your launder your loose covers in a washing machine, make sure the fabric is machine-washable.

Regularly vacuuming your curtains and blinds as well as your loose covers will go a long way towards keeping them clean and reducing the need for machine- or dry-cleaning. Be sure to use an appropriate short-bristled upholstery or other brush attachment on the hose of your vacuum cleaner and always vacuum both the front and the back of curtains and blinds.

Preparing Your Fabric

Before starting any soft-furnishing project, make sure the grain of the fabric is straight by pulling a thread across the width fabric near one of the cut ends. This is especially important with curtains or bed hangings with patterned fabric to ensure the patterns do not hang askew. If there's any problem with the grain, or if the pattern is not aligned on the grain or the pattern is not in register or is smudged, return the fabric to the supplier (before you cut it). For curtains in particular, it is also wise to remove the selvages of many fabrics before seaming, as they are prone to pucker and may spoil the clean lines of your curtain panels.

If you prefer not to remove the selvages when making soft furnishings, you can cut notches into the allowance every few centimetres/inches to prevent the seams from puckering. Leaded drapery weights sewn into the seam allowance at the hem in the corners and between joined widths can also help control vertical stitch tension in curtains. To ensure sheer fabrics hang, you can put chain or beaded weights in the hem.

Directory of Fabric Types

Acetate: A soft synthetic fabric made of cellulose acetate or acetate rayon fibre.

Awning fabrics: Durable, water-repellent, fade-resistant, synthetic, or blended outdoor fabrics, often with a flame-retardant finish.

Baize: Lightweight, felted wool cloth, usually green, that's used to line drawers, cover the bottom of lamp bases, or on billiard tables.

Batiste: A fine, soft, sheer, plain woven, cotton fabric

Basket weave: A cloth woven from two or more threads, interlaced like the weave of a basket.

Bouclé: A heavy-weight fabric with a nubby, looped surface, appropriate for upholstery.

Broadcloth: A tightly woven lustrous cotton cloth with fine embedded crosswise ribs. It resembles poplin.

Brocade: A rich jacquard-woven silk fabric with raised patterns.

Brocatelle: A brocade in which the design is woven in high relief.

Broderie anglaise: A cotton fabric, normally white or pastel colours, with a lacy embroidered pattern, often cut out. It is frequently used as a trim for pillowcases and cushions.

Buckram: A stiffened cloth, made of cotton or linen, which is used to reinforce curtain headings and pelmets. It is also known as crinoline.

Burlap: A plain woven, coarse fabric of jute, hemp, or similar natural fibres.

Calico: A plain woven, cotton cloth sometimes printed with a figured pattern, usually on one side.

Cambric: A finely woven, white, linen or cotton fabric.

Candlewick: A fabric in which loops of soft yarn are cut to produce a tufted pattern.

Canvas: A rugged, closely woven, plain woven, cotton fabric. Also known as duck.

Chambray: A plain woven fabric made of colour warp yarn and white weft yarn.

Chenille: A fuzzy, cotton yarn or fabric that has a thick pile.

Chintz: A printed, cotton fabric, glazed to give it a slightly shiny finish, usually in bright colours.

Corduroy: A cotton, ribbed, pile fabric. Comes in various weights and weaves.

Crinoline: A stiff, coarse cotton material for interlining. Also known as buckram.

Damask: A reversible fabric made from linen, silk, cotton, or wool fibres, woven with a stylized pattern, usually a foliage motif. The patterns may also be printed on any plain woven fabric.

Denim: A rugged, durable twill fabric that is most popularly dyed indigo-blue.

Dobby cloth: A fabric woven to produce small geometric patterns.

Domett: A type of baize in which the warp is cotton and the weft wool.

Duck cloth: A rugged plain-woven cloth. Also known as canvas.

Faille: A soft, transversely ribbed fabric of silk, rayon, or cotton.

Felt: A non-woven fabric of wool fibres matted together by heat, moisture, and pressure.

Flannel: A plain woven cloth, heavily brushed for softness. Often used in dressmaking and sheets.

Gauze: Thin and often transparent fabric made from any fibre in a plain or leno weave.

Greige goods (pronounced grey): Loom-state cloth that has not received wet and dry finishing.

Interlock: Double-knit, plain-stitched fabric, the same on both sides.

Jacquard: Any fabric that's made on a Jacquard loom. This type of loom

Acrylic Indoor/Outdoor

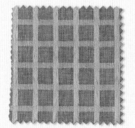
Basketweave

Chenille

Chintz

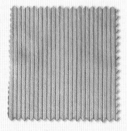
Corduroy

Damask (print)

Damask (woven)

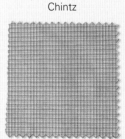
Dobby

produces elaborate cloth weaves such as tapestries, brocade, and damask.

Jersey: A single-knit, plain-stitched fabric that has a face side which is distinctly different in texture and appearance from the reverse side.

Lace: A fine, openwork fabric often used for trimmings. Lace is usually white or cream and traditionally made from cotton.

Lawn: A thin or sheer, linen or cotton fabric, that may be either plain colours or printed.

Linen: A fabric woven from flax yarn.

Madras cotton: A brightly coloured, low-cost Indian cotton fabric woven in striped or tartan patterns.

Matelassé: A woven fabric in which the pattern stands out to give a quilted look. Used in bedspreads and other soft furnishing projects.

Micro-suede: Stretch faux suede with the appearance and feel of real leather suede.

Moquette: A fabric with a thick, velvety pile, mainly used for carpets and upholstery.

Muslin: A cotton fabric made in various degrees of coarseness and often printed, woven, or embroidered with patterns. Often used for sheets.

Net: A lace-like fabric with a uniform mesh made from cotton, silk, rayon, or nylon. Net is often used to form the backing for lace.

Organdie: A fine, plain woven, sheer, cotton fabric.

Percale: A smooth, finely combed woven sheeting fabric that has a minimum thread count of 180 threads per square inch.

Poplin: A fabric with a fine horizontal rib effect on the surface because the warp yarn is finer than the filling yarn; usually a high-thread-count cloth.

Plissé: Fabric that has been treated with a caustic solution that shrinks parts of the surface to create a crinkled or pleated effect.

Sailcloth: A lightweight canvas or canvas-like fabric that is used especially for curtains.

Sateen: A strong cotton fabric constructed in satin weave with a smooth, lustrous surface; useful as a lining fabric.

Seersucker: A plain woven cotton, rayon, or linen fabric that is crinkled during the weaving process; traditionally with alternating stripes.

Sheeting: Plain woven, carded yarn cloth in medium and heavy weights. When the thread count is low, sheeting is defined as muslin. When the thread count is high and the yarn is combed, sheeting is called percale.

Taffeta: A crisp, smooth, plain-woven fabric with a slight sheen, made of various fibres, such as silk, rayon, or nylon.

Terry towelling: A cotton fabric with moisture-absorbing, loop pile covering the entire surface on one or both sides.

Ticking: A strong, tightly woven fabric of cotton or linen, used to make pillow and mattress covers.

Toile: A pattern-cut cotton fabric, sometimes used as lining.

Toile de Jouy: A traditional print in one colour, usually red, blue, yellow, or black, on a white or cream-coloured background. The prints typically feature pastoral scenes of romantic rustic figures and foliage. They were originally made in the 18th century at a factory in Jouy-en-Josas, France.

Twill: An incredibly versatile fabric identified by the diagonal lines on its face side.

Union: A sturdy fabric made with a mixture of fibres, such as cotton and linen, for greater wear.

Velour: A heavy-weight fabric with a thick warp pile that lies in several directions, producing a velvet-like appearance.

Velvet: A fabric made of any of various fibres including cotton, silk, and rayon. It has short, densely woven cut pile, which gives it a soft, rich texture.

Velveteen: A cotton pile fabric resembling velvet with a shorter pile.

Voile: A lightweight, semi-sheer fabric of wool, silk, rayon, or cotton constructed in a plain weave.

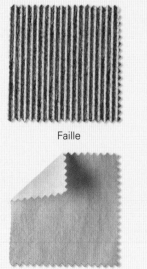

Faille

Jacquard

Matelassé

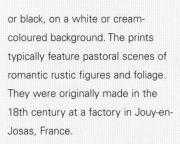

Microsuede

Napped Sateen Lining

Poplin

Silk Taffeta

Voile

techniques

Basic Sewing Kit

Whether you're a beginner or a seasoned sewer, you'll need to have a basic collection of essential tools on hand before starting any sewing project. First and foremost you'll need a sewing machine, and it's important to have a dedicated workspace. You'll need good light and a large work surface for rolling out, measuring, and cutting fabrics, especially the larger panels required for curtains and other big home decor projects.

Measuring and marking tools are an essential part of any sewer's basic kit, together with needles, pins, thread, fabric glues, and fasteners. To begin with, a few basic items is all you'll really need; it is worth getting good quality equipment made by recognized manufacturers. However, new gadgets and devices are continually being developed to make specialized tasks easier to perform. As you gain experience, you may find that these can become reliable assets in your kit, too.

The basic tools as well as some of the fancier devices are as follows:

Sewing machine: This, of course, is the most important component in your basic kit. High quality sewing machines that perform the sewing techniques required for the projects in this book are available at a wide range of prices. The more costly models offer special stitches and integrated problem-solving software, which helps you select the tension and stitch length for different fabrics and stitches. With the more affordable machines you have to control these functions manually.

Most sewing machines come with an array of sewing machine feet (see pages 178–9) that enable you to perform certain kinds of tasks, for example, ruffling, edge stitching, overcast stitching, buttonholing, and hemming, with ease and surefire accuracy. You will also need a supply of sewing machine needles for different types of materials and stitches.

If you're purchasing a new machine, be sure to read through the user's guide thoroughly before you start on any project. Practise threading the needle, filling and threading the bobbin, changing the needles and feet, and working with the attachments on a variety of fabrics. Before starting a new project, always try stitching a sample of the fabric you are going to work with and adjust stitch tension if necessary. Also, always use appropriate sewing machine needles for the project or material you're working with, replacing dull, bent, or broken needles as needed.

Keep your machine clean and store it in a dry place. Also have it oiled and serviced professionally when necessary.

Measuring tools:
Precise measuring tools are essential to the success of any sewing project. At the very least, you'll need a tape measure and a wooden or metal metre or yard stick. Metal or fibreglass tape measures are more accurate than fabric or vinyl-coated ones, both of which stretch over time. Some tape measures give measurements in reverse, too, so you can read them in either direction. There are also extra-long tape measures that extend up to 3.5m (12ft) or more, which are especially useful for larger projects.

In addition to the basic devices, there are several other measuring tools that can make your sewing project easier. A sewing gauge, which is a 15cm (6in) metal ruler with a sliding right angled guide, is handy for measuring and marking everything from buttonhole placements to seam allowance widths. To space buttonholes evenly, you can also use an accordion-fold metal gauge.

For measuring and marking lines over extended lengths, gridded table pads or large plastic cutting mats can be helpful. T-squares can also help you to keep cutting lines straight and square over a long expanse, and enable you to easily mark true right angles. Larger metal T-squares, used by carpenters and graphic designers, are useful for large-scale projects or squaring off long fabric panels on the true grain. Small 15cm (6in) and 30cm (12in) T-squares, made from transparent plastic, are great for smaller projects.

An extendable compass is useful for making circular shapes. A flexible ruler is ideal if you need to measure curved or irregularly shaped lines.

There are other tools available that allow you to measure while you sew. These include self-stick clear perspex seam gauges or adjustable plastic guides that can be screwed to the sewing machine throat plate.

For help with accurate hem measurements, consider buying a special transparent ruler that has slots for marking or pinning, or a set of metal clamps that measure and tack a hem in one step. You can even buy rulers for measuring and marking shark's teeth, scallops, and ruching, as well as geometric shapes, angles, bias strips, mitred corners, and squared-off fabric panels. Ironing aids often include handy measuring features, such as board covers printed with grids, bias lines, circles, and squares, which fit standard and tabletop ironing boards.

Marking tools: Dressmaker's or tailor's chalk is a clay chalk that comes in many colours and allows you to make marks that brush off easily from fabric. White is the easiest chalk to remove. But be sure to test a fabric scrap before you use it to make sure it doesn't stain. You can also use special fabric marking pens, which are either water- or air-soluble. Test these, too, to make sure the ink will not stain.

Another option for marking patterns is to use special coloured tracing paper and a tracing wheel. Place the tracing paper between the fabric and pattern template so that the transfer colour faces the fabric. Run the wheel along the pattern template to transfer the mark onto the fabric. The tracing paper comes in a variety of colours, some of which leave a permanent mark. Some newer tracing papers leave removable markings. Wheels with serrated and stiletto edges, are the best, but use tracing wheels with smooth edges if you are working with extremely delicate fabric.

Cutting tools: For any sewing project, a good-quality pair of dressmaking scissors is essential, as is a small pair of embroidery scissors. Choose bent-handled scissors as these allow the fabric to lie flat while you are cutting. Most people prefer scissors that are 17.5–20cm (7–8in) in length. You'll also need a pair of 10–12.5cm (4–5in) embroidery scissors or tailor point scissors for clipping and trimming fabric and for hand sewing. Pinking shears are useful for finishing off raw edges, but they dull quickly and are hard to sharpen.

Only use your scissors for cutting fabric. Keep them dry to avoid corrosion, and wipe lint from the blades frequently. Have the blades sharpened often; dull blades can damage the scissors as well as the fabric. Also, oil the hinge or pivot point now and then.

There are also several rotary cutting tools that enable you to measure as you cut and to cut several layers of fabric at the same time. Rotary cutting systems consist of a cutter, mat, and transparent ruler. Most mats and all rulers are calibrated, usually in a grid. Mats that are 75 x 90cm (30 x 36in) or larger are useful for home decorating projects because they're sized to accommodate large fabric widths. However, some people keep a 15cm (6in) square mat next to their sewing machine for spot trimming.

Needles and pins: A variety of good-quality needles and pins is essential for any sewing project. You will need hand-sewing needles in several sizes, as well as darning needles, and embroidery needles. There are also special curved needles for upholstery work and others for buttons. Hand-sewing needles need to be sharp for smooth, easy hand-stitching. Not only are dull needles difficult to work with, they cause thread to fray and material to snag.

You should also have a supply of high-quality fine-point dressmaking pins. Steel pins are best as they are rust-resistant so won't mark the fabric. Longer pins with glass or plastic heads can be easier to see on patterned fabrics and are easier to find when you drop them. Always throw away any pin that is dull, bent, or has a burr, as like needles, they snag and ruin fine fabrics. Test for burrs by running the pin along the edge of your fingernail. Always remove pins as

quickly as possible from your work to keep them from leaving holes in your fabric. T-pins are long pins with a short T-shaped top. They are useful for securing paper patterns, muslin, or fabric pieces for loose covers for chairs and sofas.

Keep your needles and pins in specially designed boxes. This will make them easier to find and it prevents them from becoming dull.

Thread: Whether you're sewing by hand or by machine, always choose a high-quality thread. Inexpensive thread tends to fray and produce lint that clogs up the inside of your sewing machine, preventing it from functioning properly. Use a thread that is appropriate for your fabric and your task. For example, choose a cotton tacking thread for tacking, synthetic thread for synthetic fabrics, and natural thread for natural fabrics. Ideally, choose linen thread for linen, and silk thread for silk, or at least use a natural fibre thread on these fabrics. Never use a synthetic thread on fabric made of natural fibres, as this type of thread can damage the fabric. Do not use cotton thread on synthetics, as cotton can shrink and cause the fabric to pucker.

In addition, choose a thread with the appropriate weight for the fabric. Light-weight fabrics, such as sheers, muslins, or voiles need a light-gauge thread, a medium-weight cotton canvas or twill requires medium-weight thread, and heavy-weight fabrics, such as denim or velvet, need strong threads.

Select a thread colour that matches your fabric, or for patterned fabrics, choose a thread to matches the dominant colour.

Notions: Always keep a pack of needle threaders handy. Even if you are good at threading needles, there is always that difficult or heavy-duty thread that can be

challenging to get through the eye of the needle without the help of this handy device. Some people also pull their thread across the edge of some beeswax before they thread it. This lightly coats the thread, strengthening it and preventing it twisting during hand sewing.

Also, keep a thimble in your kit for hand-sewing work to protect your middle finger, especially if you are working with heavy or dense fabrics. Choose a metal thimble and be sure it fits properly. Leather or plastic thimble pads with adhesive backs are an alternative.

A seam ripper is another helpful tool that enables you to pick apart seams when necessary. This has a sharp smooth point and a razor sharp curved cutting edge. Choose seam rippers with flat handles as these are less likely to roll onto the floor.

A standard pincushion can be helpful for temporarily stowing pins while working on a project. Magnetic pincushions, which are essentially large magnetic disks, are an alternative – you can just drop the pins on the disk and they'll stick without slipping.

An indispensable gadget is a bodkin. This small tool looks like a miniature set of tongs that lock into place; it is used to thread elastic, cord, or ribbon through a casing.

Fabric adhesives and fasteners: There are a number of fabric adhesives, no-sew fusible webbing materials, and other fastening devices that can all be pressed into service for soft furnishing projects.

Touch-and-close or hook-and-loop tape, for example Velcro, allows you to attach a sewn fabric element, such as a sink skirt or pelmet to another surface, such as a porcelain sink bowl or mounting board, or make soft furnishings simple to remove for cleaning. The tape consists of two separate strips of synthetic material – one of which is looped and the other hooked – these become firmly joined when pressed together, but can also easily be pulled apart. You can buy sew-on and iron-on variations in several widths and colours. It is also available in small circles or tab formats for spot fastening.

Fabric glues can be helpful for securing braids, ribbon, or trims to the edges of a pelmet or lampshade, for example.

There are various no-sew fusible webbing materials, which come in large sheets that can be cut to size, or in rolls in various widths. They enable you to iron on a tape or braid before sewing, or hem fabric without any sewing at all. Other iron-on webbing, fabric stiffeners, and pull-away stabilizers can be helpful for keeping pelmets and other soft furnishings crisp or embroidery work stable. Be sure to test any of these items on a scrap piece of fabric before you use them, as they can mark or discolour some fabrics. If this does happen the joins can be concealed or disguised with trim.

Tacking tape, a thin double-sided tape, is handy for temporarily holding fabric, zips, and trims in place until they are permanently stitched into position. It lets you re-position them until you get all the elements in the right place and holds more smoothly and consistently than pins. It's also very useful in matching stripes and plaids.

Zips, poppers, and hooks-and-eyes are among the many fastening devices available for closing sewn openings in various soft furnishings. Be sure to choose zip sizes and types that are appropriate for your fabric and project, and choose a zip with a fibre content that matches your fabric. Poppers and hooks-and-eyes are often pre-mounted on strips of binding, which can spare you from the trouble of aligning and attaching each one. Though you do still need to align the tape correctly.

Extras: There are many other helpful tools that can make projects easier. An embroidery hoop helps stabilize hand-embroidered details. An embroiderer's magnifying glass makes fine detailed stitching easier to see.

Twill tape or ring tape can simplify the construction of Roman blinds, and curtain heading tapes enable you to make any number of pleated curtain headings quickly and easily. A staple gun is useful for attaching fabric to wood or board, such as when you are making blinds or pelmets, and a tacking gun enables you to fix pleats together or attach blind rings with plastic fasteners.

Tissue-like pattern paper or brown paper can help you make custom patterns for chair cushions and loose covers, or scalloped or shaped edges for valances or table cloths. Graph paper is invaluable for plotting scale versions of designs up or down.

A large knitting needle can be helpful in turning tabs or ties right side out. A point turner, usually made of plastic or bamboo, can be used to push out corners and points without making holes in the fabric. A Fasturn cylinder – a specially designed device – and interchangeable hooks in various sizes also ease the turning of ties and tabs.

Pattern weights can make cutting faster than pinning. But you'll need to be careful as weights don't hold your fabric as firmly as pins. You can buy special weights but you can also make your own. Cans of food can make fine weights, and small bottles or containers filled with rice or stones are ideal. A third hand, or bird and clamp, is also useful when you need extra help to hold a fabric in place. It is a spring-closed clip, which can be attached to a table by a screw-fixed clamp.

Finally, a must in the basic sewing kit is a good iron and ironing board. Proper ironing can be the key to the success of any project. You'll need to iron out any creases in your fabric before you begin measuring and cutting. Check the fibre content of your fabric, put the iron on the correct setting, and test on a small piece before following through on your main piece of fabric. Certain fabrics, such as cotton or linen, need to be steamed, or pressed through a damp cloth, others, including silk, should not be pressed with steam as they'll shrink or flatten out.

Hand-sewing Techniques

Although there are professionals who insist on hand-sewing everything from hems to pleats to headings, sewing machines, especially the newer models with their wide array of pre-programmed integrated stitches, make most sewing tasks for home decor projects much simpler. Nonetheless, certain aspects of most projects have to be done by hand. For instance, before machine-stitching certain seams or hems, you should tack the fabric, and often the lining in place temporarily beforehand. The following basic hand stitches can be useful for finishing all kinds of home furnishing projects; many of them are used in the projects in this book.

Running Stitch

The simplest of hand stitches is the running stitch. It involves making small, even stitches along both sides of the fabric, by simply pulling the needle up from the back, then down through the front and up again through the back and so forth to produce a straight line of stitches. Running stitches are used to gather fabrics, which you can do by wrapping

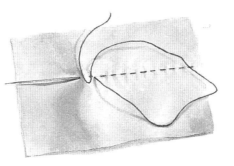

the ends of the line of stitches around pins and pulling the thread with even pressure from both sides.

A variation of the running stitch is used for temporarily fixing, or tacking, fabrics together. For tacking, however, the stitches are longer on the working side of the fabric and shorter on the back of the fabric. As the tacking stitches will be removed later it's helpful to use a contrasting thread so that they are easier to see.

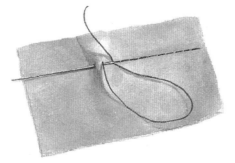

Backstitch

The backstitch is a small, strong stitch that may be used as an alternative to machine seaming or for small, difficult-to-access areas. To produce this stitch, bring the needle up through the back of the fabric, make a stitch backwards (first stitch), then bring your needle up just beyond the beginning of the first stitch (about half a stitch's length). Take the needle back to the end of the first stitch, insert it here (second stitch), then pull it up again just in front of the beginning of the second stitch – again about half a stitch's length. Continue in the same way until your stitch line is complete. Using two or three backstitches on top of each other is a useful way to finish off other types of hand stitches.

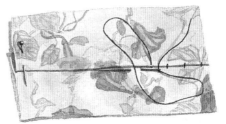

Ladder Stitch

A ladder stitch is ideal when you need to join two pieces of fabric and match a pattern across a seam. Before working this stitch, press under the seam allowance to the wrong side along one edge. With the right sides of the fabric facing up, place the folded edge on top of the other piece of fabric, matching the pattern and pinning in place at right angles to the folded edge, With the fabrics still facing up, insert the needle through the very edge of the fold, take a small stitch across the lower layer along the join, then insert the needle again through the edge of the fold, repeating this sequence until the fabrics are joined. On small areas, this stitch may be used as the final stitching, for larger areas it can be used as a tacking stitch before sewing a flat seam.

Slipstitch

A slipstitch holds two folded seam allowances together to close an opening in a machine-stitched seam, for example, or to finish mitred corners (see page 176). With the allowances folded and pressed to the wrong side, place the two folded edges parallel to each, abutting the folds. Working on the right side of the fabric from right to left, slip the needle

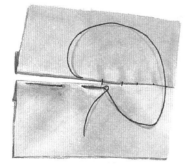

through the fold of one piece of fabric, secure the thread with a couple of backstitches, then take a small 6mm (¼in) stitch inside the fold, bring the needle out of the fold, then insert the needle through the fold of the adjoining fabric exactly opposite the point it emerged from on the other side, catch a few threads from this fold then bring the needle back through the other fold and repeat, making sure the fabric does not pucker as you complete the line of stitching.

Hemming Stitch

This stitch holds a folded edge of fabric flat to the fabric and can produce a neater finish than hemming by machine. Working with the wrong side up and the folded edge facing you, point the needle diagonally from right to left, bring the needle under the folded edge and up through the two layers of fabric, catch a few threads of the main fabric just above the hem. Repeat along the length of the hem. If your fabric is heavy and you want to avoid a bulky double folded hem, sew a strip of seam binding along the raw edge and sew the hemming stitch through the binding.

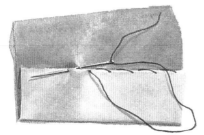

Herringbone Stitch

A herringbone or catch stitch is a flat stitch that may be used instead of hemming stitch along a raw edge. It is particularly useful for heavy or bulky fabric or along curved hems. It is also used to join the overlapping edges of wadding. Working on the wrong side of the fabric from left to right, take a horizontal stitch through the layer of flat fabric moving the needle from right to left and picking up just a couple of threads of fabric. Turn the needle towards the right and take a diagonal stitch over the raw edge of the folded fabric, then take another small horizontal stitch, again from right to left, and draw the needle up with another diagonal stitch, catching a few threads horizontally across the flat fabric from right to left; repeat making diagonal and cross stitches across the hem edge.

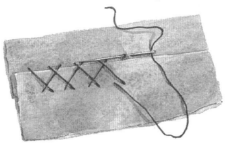

Blanket Stitch

This stitch is worked along a raw or folded edge of fabric to finish it. It is also used as a decorative stitch for appliqué work, often worked with a contrasting thread to draw attention to the stitch pattern. Working with the right side of the fabric facing up, fasten the thread just under the edge of the fabric, then draw the needle through the underside of the fabric at the desired distance from the raw edge, pull the needle at a right angle towards the raw edge, looping the needle under the fastened stitch at the edge, then down through the front of the fabric about 3–6mm (⅛–¼in) from the first stitch. Insert

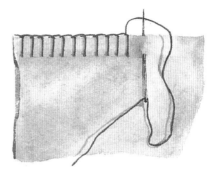

the needle from front to back to front in a single motion and before pulling the needle and thread through the fabric, carry the thread along the raw edge under the point of needle. Continue in this way, inserting the needle from front to back to front and looping the needle under the working thread before starting the next stitch all the way along the fabric edge.

Satin Stitch

Similar to blanket stitch, this stitch is used to fill in drawn shapes or it can be used to attach a cutout fabric to another piece of fabric and conceal its raw edges, and is generally worked with a contrasting embroidery thread. Make a series of small, tightly packed, straight stitches, side by side. Bring up the needle from the back of the fabric through to the front near the edge of the cutout. Pull the thread over the edge of the cutout, by 3–6mm (⅛–¼in), then draw the needle from the front through to the back. Pull your needle up from the back to the front right next to the first stitch, then insert from front to back. Continue until the shape is filled or the edge is covered.

Buttonhole Stitch

This stitch is also like the blanket stitch except the stitches are worked very closely to form a firm finished edge. It is used to finish the edges of a cut

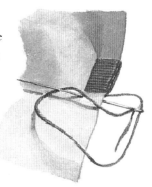

buttonhole. For extra strength, use a heavier-weight thread. Working in the opposite direction to the blanket stitch, insert the needle through the fabric at the desired distance from the raw edge, twist the working thread around the point of the needle, then pull the needle through and press the thread loop towards the raw edge so that it forms a knot along the cut edge. When you reach the corner of the buttonhole, make a bar of stitches close together in a fan shape to stop the fabric splitting, then continue as before.

Machine-sewing Techniques

Before starting any type of machine-stitching, make sure you understand the characteristics of your fabric, that the grain is straight (see page 167), the right thread has been selected (see page 171), your machine is set to the proper tension (see page 170), and the feed dogs and sewing machine foot (see page 178) are in the right position.

To eliminate bulk from seams you can trim the seam allowance close to the stitch line after sewing. Fabrics prone to fraying, should not be trimmed, as the cloth may separate from the seam. If you plan to press the seam to one side, rather than press it open, you can grade the seams by cutting just one of the seam allowances for a smoother finish.

Topstitch

This is where a straight machine stitch is used to finish off a hem. The line of stitches will be visible on the right side of the fabric.

Flat Seam

To make a flat seam, pin the two pieces of fabric to be joined together with right-sides facing, and patterns and raw edges matching. Place the pins at right angles to the raw edges at even intervals along the length of the seam.

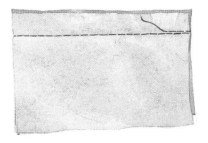

Tack along the seam 3–12mm (⅛–½in) from the raw edges, removing pins as you go. Machine alongside, but not on top of the tacking stitches (they'll be difficult to remove otherwise). Secure the line of stitching at both ends with a few reverse stitches. Remove the tacking stitches and press open the seam or press it in one direction or the other, or neaten it with pinking shears.

If you remove the selvages of your fabric and want to neaten the raw edges before seaming, use overcast stitch and an edging foot (see page 178). The allowances of fine fabrics can be turned under and hemmed by hand (see page 174), or if the fabric is bulky, you can also finish the edges of the seam allowance with seam binding.

Overlocking

Another way to finish the raw edges of a seam is to employ a technique called overlocking. To overlock a flat seam, trim the top seam allowance to about 3mm (⅛in) turn and press the other edge under by 3mm (⅛in), then turn again to enclose the trimmed raw edge. Placing the folded edge along the flat seam line, press again, and hand-hem the fabric close to the seam line (illustration above right).

French Seam

If you need to produce a totally enclosed seam with no lines of stitching showing on the right side of the fabric, join your fabric with a hard-wearing French seam. This seam is often used for pillowcases and loose covers and is useful

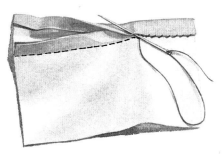

when joining fabrics that will not be concealed by lining. To make a French seam, place your fabrics with wrong sides together and raw edges matching and machine-stitch a seam about 6mm (¼in) from the raw edges. Trim the seam allowance slightly and press the edges together. Turn the fabric back over itself along the seam so the right sides are facing and the seam runs along the centre of the fold (illustration below). Tack the two layers about 12mm (½in) from the fold, then machine-stitch just inside the tacking to enclose the raw edges. Remove the tacking, then press the seam to one side on the wrong side of the fabric.

Flat-fell Seam

A flat-fell seam is another hard-wearing seam that will give a flat finish, but two parallel lines of stitches will be visible along the face of the fabric. It is used to form the inner seams of

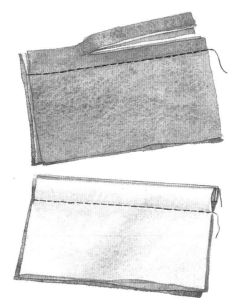

the legs of denim jeans, and for soft furnishings it is often used for bedspreads, tablecloths, or awnings, where a strong well-encased seam allowance is demanded.

To make a flat-fell seam, place the two pieces of fabric with their wrong sides together and raw edges aligned, then stitch a flat seam about 12mm (½in) from the raw edges. Press both allowances to one side; trim the lower seam allowance to about 3mm (⅛in). Turn the upper seam allowance under by 6mm (¼in) over the trimmed allowance to enclose it. Machine-stitch the top allowance to the fabric, close to the first seam line, to enclose it. Then machine-stitch another line of stitching close to the folded edge and parallel to the first line of stitching to join the enclosed seam to the front of the fabric.

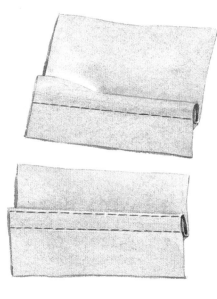

Neatening Corners and Curves

If you need to join two pieces of fabric and make right-angled corners for a pillow or cushion cover, for example, you can stitch right up to the edge of the corner and, making sure the needle is in the down position before turning the corner, lift the foot and turn the fabric through 90 degrees, then put the foot back down and continue

until you reach the next corner then repeat. Before turning the cover right-side out, trim the seam allowances at the corners. Cut the corners on the diagonal just outside the stitch line. If the corner is more acute than 90 degrees, machine-sew a few stitches across the corner point, and trim the selvage in a straight line across the pointed end beyond the stitch line (illustration above).

If you're machine-stitching a curved seam, such as a shaped headboard cover or the end of a bolster cover, cut notches into the seam at regular intervals to allow the seams to lie flat when the fabric is turned right side out.

Mitring Corners

To mitre the corners of hemmed edges, begin by folding in and pressing double hems along the edges to the desired depth (1). Unfold one of the folds of each double hem, fold in and press the corner along the diagonal and cut off the tip of the corner across the pressed edges (2). Open out the folded hem completely, fold in the corner, fold over and pin one hem over the folded corner (3), then repeat for the other so that the folded edges of each hem meet in a neat mitred fold at the corner. Finish the fold by hand with slipstitch (4). Machine-stitch to hem the edges or hand-sew with hemming stitch.

Piping and Binding

The seams or perimeter edges of many soft furnishings can be given a neat finish and professional polish with piping or binding.

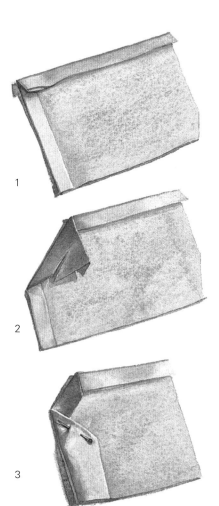

Readymade piping can be purchased as cord with an attached lip, and readymade bias binding or straight binding is also available in a variety of widths and colours. However, most readymades are made of thin fabrics in narrow widths and are best for smaller projects in lightweight fabrics. You may also make piping and binding yourself with matching or contrasting fabrics. Since piping coverings and bindings are cut on the bias, interesting results can be achieved with striped or checked fabrics.

Making piping: To make covered piping, you'll need to cut several strips of fabric on the bias, each wide enough to cover your cord, and allow for a 12mm (½in) lip along the seam allowance. Choose a piping cover or binding fabric that is similar in weight and fibre to your main fabric. Make sure it is shrink-resistant and colourfast to keep it from damaging the main fabric when you launder it. Cord comes in several diameters, so make the width of your bias strips equal to the diameter of the cord plus 2.5cm (1in). Before you wrap your cord, shrink it by soaking it for five minutes in clean boiling water, then leave it to dry. If you don't shrink the cord first, it will shrink when you wash your cover and cause the piping to pucker.

Cutting a piping cover on the bias, makes it more flexible and it will have more "give" around corners. To find the true bias of a fabric, fold a straight raw edge at an angle across the fabric to align with a selvage edge. The angled fold line at the side of the triangle is the true bias and will serve as a baseline. Using a ruler and tailor's chalk or a marking pen, mark strips of fabric equal to the desired width, parallel to the baseline, then cut them out. You'll need to cut enough fabric strips to cover the finished length of piping or binding, including the seams that will join them.

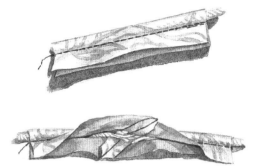

To join the strips into a continuous cover, place two strips together at right angles, right sides facing and raw edges aligned. Pin then machine-stitch to join them with a 12mm (½in) seam (illustration below left). Continue joining the pieces in this way until you have the length you need, press open and trim the seams. Then place the cover right-side down on a work surface. Position the cord along the centre of the cover and wrap the cover around the cord. Tack to close the cover (illustration above), then machine-stitch it using a piping or zipper foot (see page 178).

When you're ready to sew the piping into the seam of your project, place the fabric face up on a work surface, align the raw edges of the piping with the raw edges of the fabric panel and pin then tack the two together. Place the second panel over the first, trapping the piping between, and pin then tack all layers together. Machine-stitch all three layers together, using a piping foot or zipper foot as close to the cord as possible (illustration below). To make a smooth join at the ends of the piping on your finished project, unravel the ends of the cord a bit, intertwine them, fold the ends of the piping cover over the

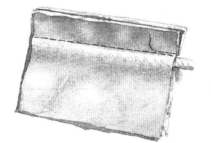

twine, folding one end under to cover the raw edge of the other and hand sew to finish. Remove your tacking and turn right side out.

Making binding: If you want to make bias binding, make a continuous strip of several pieces of fabric cut on the bias as described above for the piping cover. Fold in and press both long raw edges by 3–6mm (⅛–¼in) towards the wrong side of the fabric.

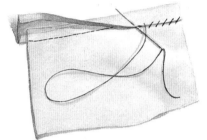

To sew the binding onto the main fabric by hand, open one folded edge of the binding and match it to the raw edge of the fabric with right sides together. Pin in place then backstitch the layers together along the fold line of the binding. Fold the binding back down, then fold and press it around the raw edge of the fabric, pin it in place, and sew the second folded edge to the back of the fabric using hemming stitch (illustration above).

To sew the binding by machine, fold and press the binding in half lengthwise towards the wrong side and place and pin it over the raw edge of the fabric to be bound. Tack the binding to the fabric, then machine-stitch close to both folded edges of the binding. Remove your tacking stitches.

Sewing Machine Feet

There are several sewing machine feet attachments that can help make various aspects of sewing projects easier and help you to achieve more professional-looking results.

Adjustable blind hem foot: This type of foot (right) can be moved from side to side to fine tune the amount of fabric caught by the blind hemstitch. One side of the foot is raised to float just above the folded edge, while the lower side glides along the fabric. See your sewing machine manual for instructions on how to make a blind hem on your machine.

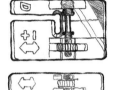

Adjustable buttonhole foot: This particular foot has a slide that is adjustable for different sizes of buttons. Buttonhole feet vary with different machine brands.

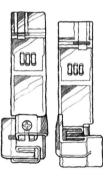

Bias binder: Available in various sizes, this foot (left) enables edges to be easily bound with bias binding.

Candlewicking foot: This foot has a deep tunnel on the underside that enables it to be fed over a built-up decorative French Knot-type stitch in order to create an heirloom candlewicking effect.

Clear Edge Joining Foot: This foot guides decorative stitching over a seam, trim, ribbon, or marked line. A tunnel on the bottom allows the stitches to form perfectly and the flange in the centre keeps stitches aligned with the seam line.

Clear piping foot: This foot has a shaped bottom edge and is see-through to allow you to view the piping placement and stitching easily, which means you can get as close to the covered cord as possible.

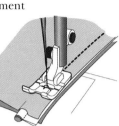

Edging foot: This foot is used for overcast stitching to bind a raw side edge that might be puckered or curled by the stitches. A tiny wire on the edge of the foot prevents the curling of the fabric edge as it is stitched.

Edge guide: This attachment is used for wide seam allowances, pin tuck, channel quilting, or even topstitching.

Edge stitching foot: This foot guides topstitching and edge-stitching perfectly and allows folded tucks to be stitched accurately.

Gathering foot: This type of foot (below) allows you to gather fabric and attach a ruffle in one step.

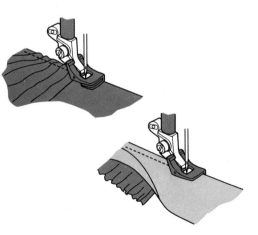

Hemmer: This foot rolls a 10mm (⅓in) double hem in light- to medium-weight fabrics and hems with a straight stitch.

Hemstitch fork: This attachment allows you to stitch seams with a decorative open work stitch that looks hand-sewn.

Left edge topstitch foot: The left edge topstitch foot (below) perfectly guides your topstitching and edge stitching. The underside of the foot is designed to glide along the folded edge of the fabric to give you a beautifully even topstitch. It is great for hemming bulky projects such as curtains, as it allows the bulk of the fabric to be placed to the left of the free arm for easier sewing.

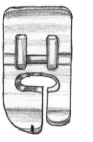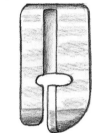

Narrow hem foot: This foot is great for making narrow hems on napkins, curtains, and ruffles in medium-weight fabrics.

Narrow zipper foot: This foot (below) allows you to stitch extra close to zip teeth, poppers, popper tape, beads, and other elements. It can be snapped on to the right or left of the needle, and the grooves on the underside grip speciality fabrics for excellent feeding.

Piping foot: The shape of this foot enables you to sew close to the covered cord for a neat edge and tailored finish.

Roller foot: This type of foot allows you to smoothly sew leathers, velvets, and fabrics with naps or loops or at uneven levels. It allows for straight, zigzag, and other forward-motion utility and decorative stitches.

Ruffler: The ruffler foot creates small pleats or gathers light- to medium-weight fabrics.

Shell rolled hem foot: This foot enables you to stitch a rolled hem in sheer and very lightweight fabrics

Single welt cord foot: This foot allows you to accurately make and insert welt cord into loose covers and other soft furnishing projects. It sews like a piping foot, but is designed for larger cord.

Spanish hemstitch foot: Allows a Spanish hemstitch to be perfectly sewn between two folded edges. This is an heirloom sewing attachment.

Measuring Up

The old carpenter's adage "measure twice, cut once" is equally applicable to sewing projects. Whether you're making cushions or curtains, each step goes much more smoothly and the final product will fit perfectly when you check and recheck the measurements. Always use a metal tape measure or metal or wooden metre (yard) stick. It also helps to have someone to assist you on complicated projects, to hold one end of the tape and to double check your measurements. Make an annotated sketch on graph paper including all your measurements to take to the fabric retailer (see pages 164–7 for advice on choosing suitable fabrics).

Curtains

When you are measuring up for curtains, it is best if the curtain rail, pole, or track is already mounted in the desired position. At the least

you need to know how wide it will be and its exact position over the window, as well as the precise diameter of the pole, if relevant.

Basic width and drop: The main two measurements required for calculating fabric quantity are the width and drop of the finished treatment. In most cases, you'll want to put the pole well above the top of the window frame, either near the ceiling or just under the cornice if you have any, or halfway between the top of the frame and ceiling or the base of the cornice. The rail should also extend well beyond the sides of the window frame to allow the fabric panels to fold back without blocking much of the window.

The more space you have around the window, the more well-proportioned the window treatment will be. If there is no wall space beside the window, a blind may be a better solution. If you have wall space only on one side of the window, consider a single curtain that can be tied back to one side.

Other considerations: The type of pole or track you'll be using, as well as the type of heading and top treatment will also affect your measurements. For ceiling-mounted traverse tracks, measure the entire width of the track and add 7.5cm (3in) for a pair of curtains to overlap in the middle. For wall-mounted tracks with returns, measure the width of the track, plus the returns, plus the overlap. If you are mounting your curtains from a rod or pole, measure the length of the rod, excluding the finials (but be sure to include the finials in your calculation before you purchase the rod to be sure everything fits.) To determine the drop measurement of the finished treatment, decide whether your curtains will hang level with, just above, or just below the track or pole, and calculate from this point to the bottom of the window sill or

to the floor, depending on how long you want your curtains. And if you want your curtains to break, or puddle, at the floor, add the extra to your drop calculation. Also, be sure to take into consideration the flooring if it has not yet been installed. Thick carpets or raised floors can have a substantial impact on your drop measurement.

Other measurements to consider are the projection depth of any brackets that fix the curtain pole, and the width and depth of any radiator or other built-in element below the window. Consider too, the depth of the window frame moulding and the sill, and any other obstructions, such as pipes or sockets, which might affect your choice of treatment.

Allowances: After you've noted the finished width and drop measurements of your curtains, add the allowances for turnings and hems. You'll need to add between 12.5–40cm (5–16in) on the length. A fairly deep double hem – about 10cm (4in) – is desirable for an elegant drape of floor-length curtains; for double-height spaces, you can double the depth to about 20cm (8in), depending on the weight of the fabric. Also, depending on the type of heading you're planning, allow 5–25cm (2–10in) for turning at the top.

Heading and fullness: The heading and fullness of your curtains as well as the width of the fabric and the size of any pattern repeat will also affect the amount of fabric you'll need. Deep or quadruple pleats require extra fabric, while certain gathered or flat panels will need less. Don't scrimp on fullness – skimpy curtains detract from rather than add to a room. Calculate the width you need by including a fullness factor of 1½ to 3 times the length of the curtain rail for each panel. Then calculate the number of widths of fabric joined together that you'll need to achieve this desired fullness.

Pattern repeats: If your fabric is patterned, you'll need to purchase enough extra fabric to be able to match the patterns. To determine how much extra fabric you'll need, find out the measurements of the repeat, which is typically listed on the manufacturer's label, or you can find it yourself by measuring from top to bottom and from side to side of a complete recurring pattern. Divide the total cut drop measurement by the height of the pattern repeat and round up to a whole number of repeats. Each width needs to include the same number of repeats so the patterns match when the curtains are drawn. It is also best to ensure you include a complete motif at the hem – allow sufficient fabric to create a deep double hem below this bottom motif. Finally, to ensure that you'll be able to choose where the motif falls, buy enough fabric for one extra repeat for each width. (See also Working with Patterns, page 165.)

Blinds

Measurements for blinds depend on whether your treatment will be mounted inside or outside the window frame and the style of blind. Simple Roman blinds hang as flat panels when opened, and require the least fabric; hobbled Roman blinds require 2–3 times the length to allow for the built-in soft folds; and Austrian blinds require more width to create layers of generous folds.

Whether your blind is mounted inside or outside the frame, it will be fixed to a rod or batten, which determines its finished width. If you're measuring for an inside-mounted blind, take into consideration the recess of the window, as well as the depth and type the frame. The depth of the frame determines the position of your batten – it should fit neatly within the frame, while still allowing the blind to be let down over any latches or projecting frames of lower sash windows. Avoid screwing battens into metal or PVC window frames. For deeply recessed windows, mount the shade as close to the window as possible.

Inside-mounted: To measure for an inside-mounted blind, measure from side to side inside the frame at the top, middle, and bottom of the window, and note any differences. In older houses, frames may be slightly askew or have settled unevenly over time. In order for the finished blind to drop evenly over the length of the window, it will need to be slightly shorter than the shortest width measurement: subtract about 12mm (½in) from the shortest width of the inside of the frame to get the finished width of the blind – this will leave about 6mm (¼in) of breathing room on either side of the mounted blind. To calculate the drop of the finished blind, measure from the top of the inside of the frame to the top of the window sill.

Outside-mounted: Blinds that are mounted outside the window recess will be secured to the wall with L-shaped brackets attached to the batten, or to the ceiling with screws and wall anchors. So begin by determining the cut length and position of the mounting board or batten. The batten should be positioned either several inches above the top of the frame to allow room for the L-shaped brackets, or just below the bottom of the cornice. It should also extend anywhere from 12mm (½in) to several centimetres/inches beyond the side edges of the window frame so that the side edges of the blind completely cover the window

Measuring windows

Take note of the following measurements when planning curtains and blinds.

1   Length of curtain or blind fixture
2   Stack back (extension of fixture beyond window)
3   Drop from fixture to sill
4   Drop from fixture to radiator
5   Drop from fixture to floor
6   Distance from fixture to ceiling
7   Distance from fixture to top of window
8   Height or depth of window (with no recess)
9   Height or depth of window (inside recess)
10 Width of window (with no recess)
11 Width of window (inside recess)

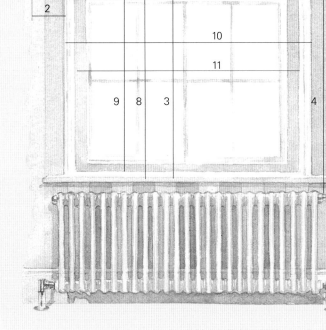

frame, the sill projection, and/or any L-shaped brackets that may need to be mounted outside the sides of the frame. (It's best to avoid mounting the board directly onto the front of the window frame.) Measure the cut width of the board or batten to determine the cut width of the finished blind, and measure from the top of the planned position of the mounting board to the sill to determine the finished length of the blind.

Blind design: To calculate the cut dimensions and the amount of fabric you'll need for a standard Roman blind, add between 7.5–15cm (3–6in) for the hem and turned top edge to the drop, and add between 4–10cm (2–4in) to the finished width measurement for turning under side hems. If you will require more than one fabric width to achieve the desired finished width, remember to add seam allowances into your calculations for joining widths.

For hobbled Roman blinds, double or triple the drop, depending on the style of folds you desire, and add the allowances as for Roman blinds for hems and turnings to the drop and the width measurements.

For Austrian blinds, measure from the top of the track to the sill and add between 7.5–15cm (3–6 in) for the hem and turned top edge. The type of heading tape and the length of the track will dictate the cut width of the fabric. Add allowances for turning the side hems and any joins in the fabric if necessary.

For festoon blinds double the drop measurement to allow for the ruched effect, or triple it for really full blinds. The width is calculated as for Austrian blinds.

For a roller blind, add about 2.5cm (1in) to the width for side hems. If the fabric is pre-stiffened or will not fray, it is not necessary to add an allowance for side hems. Add about 30cm (12in) to the drop to allow for the lathe

pocket at the bottom and the attachment to the roller at the top. For outside-mounted roller blinds, you may need to mount the brackets on small pieces of wood screwed into the wall so that the blind will project enough to clear the window frame. In this case, you'll probably want to cover the top of the blind with a pelmet, valance, or other top treatment.

As for curtains, you'll need to add extra fabric for centring or matching repeats of any patterned fabrics for any type of blind (see Pattern repeats, under Curtains, opposite). See the illustration opposite for all of the additional measurements to note when measuring up windows for blinds.

Pelmets and other top treatments

Whether you're creating a top treatment to stand alone or to cover curtains panels or a blind, its positioning is crucial to the success of the overall effect.

When measuring up, start by calculating the outside width and height of the window frame. Then measure from the top of the frame to the bottom of the cornice or the ceiling itself to determine the amount of headroom you'll have for mounting the mounting board or other fixtures. Usually top treatments are mounted at least 5–25cm (2–10in) above the window frame to keep the treatment from blocking too much light at the top of the window.

If the top treatment will cover an outside-mounted blind or a set of curtains that extend well beyond the sides of the window frame, the mounting board or rod for the top treatment needs to extend beyond the edges of this under-treatment by at least 2.5–5cm (1–2in) on either side.

Other considerations: The style of the top treatment and the manner in which it is mounted will also effect your measurements. Hard cornices or lambrequins are mounted

on boards and can have a depth ⅕ to as much as ⅓ of the height of the total treatment, while soft valances over curtains are mounted on double tracks or rods and can be gathered, which requires 2–3 times the width of the rod or track to achieve the desired fullness. As for curtains and blinds, you'll need to work out the pattern repeat if the fabric has a design that needs to be joined across the width or centred across its depth (see Pattern repeats, under Curtains, opposite).

Making Loose Cover Patterns

To ensure your loose covers will fit well you can make a trial cover using muslin, calico, or some other inexpensive cloth to test the lines and the cut before using more costly fabric. Once you are sure the cover perfectly fits, you can separate the seams and use the individual pieces as your pattern. Another approach is to make a pattern from pattern paper, which is readily available from craft shops.

To make a paper or muslin pattern for upholstered furnishings, measure the front, back, seat, and sides of the piece of furniture, cut out rectangles of paper or muslin several centimetres/inches larger than the actual dimensions, and pin the paper or fabric onto the sofa or chair. For muslin patterns, trim the edges for a precise fit. For paper patterns, trace around the lines of the chair or sofa with a pencil, clipping into the paper around curves and corners. Cut off the excess paper and refit the pattern, adjusting the lines two or three times to get an accurate fit. Leave 5–10cm (2–4in) allowances around the seat for tucking in. Use the same approach to make patterns for wooden chairs, using tape to secure the paper or fabric to the chair.

Remember to match patterned fabrics from one section of the chair to the next, and to allow for cutting napped fabrics so that the nap runs in the same direction on all sides.

glossary

Accent colour: A secondary or tertiary colour in a colour scheme, usually introduced in smaller amounts to add balance to the composition.

Advancing colour: Warm colours of the spectrum, which appear to advance towards you, creating the impression of enclosing a space.

Appliqué: A layer of fabric, usually cut into a stylized motif, placed over a base fabric and attached to it with decorative edge stitching, such as satin stitch, fabric adhesive, or fusible webbing.

Apron: The wooden trim moulding below the windowsill.

Architrave: The moulding around a window or door.

Art Deco: A design movement, fashionable in the 1920s and 30s, that is characterized by geometric shapes and stylized forms.

Art Nouveau: A turn of the 19th-century style, characterized by organic shapes and flowing lines.

Arts and Crafts: A late 19th-century movement, led by William Morris, dedicated to bringing simplicity and high standards of craftsmanship into home design.

Austrian blind: A softly ruched blind, often made of a sheer fabric. It is known for its formal appearance and extravagant vertical shirring between loose scallops.

Baize: A lightweight, felted wool cloth, usually green and used for linings in drawers, on lamp bases, or on billiard tables.

Balloon blind: A blind known for the balloon-like pouffes of fabric at its base, which are visible whether the blind is up or down.

Banding: Strips of contrasting fabric sewn to the edge or hem of curtains.

Baseboard: see Skirting board.

Basting thread: see Tacking thread.

Batik: A fabric dyeing technique in which melted wax is applied to cloth, usually lightweight cotton, in various stylized designs before dyeing. When the wax is removed a rough contrasting impression remains.

Baton: A wand used to draw curtains.

Batting: see Wadding.

Bay window: A large window, or series of windows, projecting from the outer wall of a building and forming a recess within.

Beadwork: Fabric adorned with sewn bead ornamentation, often combined with embroidery work.

Bed curtains: Fabric panels positioned above and around a bed, usually used to dress a four-poster bed.

Bendable lauan: Bendable wood used for arched treatments and coronas.

Bias cut: Fabric cut at a 45-degree angle to the selvage.

Bias binding: A seamed strip of cloth made from lengths of fabric cut on the bias to give it some stretch. It is used to trim raw edges or enclose piping cord.

Blend: A term given to a fabric made of a mixture of fibres to improve handling and durability. Also, known as union cloth, a linen/cotton blend particularly popular for upholstery.

Blind: A flat, pleated, or ruched fabric window treatment positioned in front of the window pane and usually drawn up horizontally from the bottom to the top by means of cords. Also known as a shade.

Block-printing: A hand-printing process prominent in the mid-18th century, which relies on carved wooden blocks to transfer dyed motifs to fabric or papers.

Boss: A metal or wooden element attached to a wall to hold back curtains to allow light into a space, or to hold back over-bed curtains. Also called a holdback.

Bow window: Like a bay window except that the projection is curved rather than angled.

Box pleat: A flat, symmetrical pleat made by folding the fabric to the back of each side of the pleat, with two folded edges facing each other.

Braid: Woven ribbon trim used to edge blinds, trim curtains or cushions, or cover tacks on upholstered pieces.

Break: The extra length added to curtain panels so they touch the floor by 2.5cm (1in) or more.

Buckram: A coarse fabric made of cotton or jute and stiffened with sizing. It is used to reinforce the headings of curtains, or to stiffen the fabrics used in cornices, pelmets, or tiebacks.

Bullion fringe: A long silky fringe of twisted cords.

Bump: A fibrous cotton wadding used to interline drapes to add bulk. Also called interlining.

Café curtain: A half-length curtain attached to a rod or pole mounted across the middle of a window and designed to prevent passers-by from looking into a space.

Calendering: A process of passing cloth through heavy rollers to impart sheen to the surface.

Carriers: Small runners in tracks or traverse rods to which pin hooks or curtain hooks may be attached.

Cartridge pleat: A fold of cloth sewn to create fullness. It is a round pleat, often shaped around a tubular support or stuffed with buckram.

Cascade: A fall of knife-pleated, self-lined or contrast-lined fabric that descends in a zigzag formation from a top treatment. Also known as tails.

Casement window: A vertically hinged window, framed with timber or metal, and opening inwards or outwards with a crank mechanism.

Casing: A simple, double-hemmed pocket at the top of curtains, through which a rod or pole may be slotted to create a gathered heading.

Centre draw: A traversing pair of curtains that open and close from the centre of the window.

Chain weights: A chain of small beads enclosed in a fabric casing, used in the hems of lightweight curtains to keep them straight.

Chair rail: see Dado moulding.

Clearance: The distance between the back of a curtain track and the wall.

Cleat: A piece of metal or wood having projecting arms or ends around which a blind cord can be wound or secured. It is typically screwed into a window frame or wall.

Clerestory window: Vertical window set in a roof structure or high in a wall, used to introduce daylight.

Cloud blind: Like a balloon blind except that its pouffes lie straight across the bottom when it is down.

Combination rods: Two or three curtain rods on one set of brackets.

Complementary colours: A colour, opposite any given colour on a colour wheel, introduced into a colour scheme to create a dynamic effect.

Cornice: A boxed top treatment mounted above a window and often covered with fabric. A cornice can also be a type of wooden, plaster, or synthetic moulding that runs along the top of a wall next to the ceiling to disguise or adorn the join between the two surfaces.

Corona: A circular, semi-circular, or oval structure reminiscent of a crown fixed to the wall or ceiling above a bed and used to support bed curtains.

Coving: Moulding similar to a cornice but with simpler lines.

Crewelwork: An embroidery style originating in India and executed in a thin worsted yarn mostly with chain or herringbone stitches on cotton, linen, or wool. Designs typically feature foliage, vine patterns, or flowers. The technique was commonly used to adorn English and American bed hangings.

Crosswise grain: The threads of a woven fabric that run perpendicular to the selvage.

Curtain drop: The length of a curtain from the hanging system to the bottom edge of the hem.

Cut length: The cut length of curtains, which includes allowance for turning the heading at the top and the hem at the bottom.

Dado: The lower broad part of an interior wall that is finished in wallpaper, a fabric, or paint, and decorated differently from the upper section, as with panels.

Dado moulding: A wooden, plaster, or synthetic moulding positioned over the lower 90cm (3ft) or so of the walls of a room, above the baseboard moulding. Also known as a chair rail, it was devised to prevent chair backs from marring the walls.

Decorator or furnishing cotton: Natural cotton yarn woven into fabric of many qualities and weights – from upholstery fabrics to lightweight voiles – specifically for soft furnishings.

Door jamb: The top and sides of a frame against which a door closes.

Dormer window: A window projecting from and set into a sloping roof to allow light into the roof space.

Double-hung window: see Sash window.

Drapery hooks: see Pin hooks.

Draw rod: A rod inserted into the heading to open and close curtains.

Dress curtains: Curtains that are purely decorative and do not close across the window.

Duplex print: Fabric that is printed on both sides to provide a reversible pattern.

Dust ruffle: A wide ruffle encircling the bottom perimeter of a bed and reaching to the floor, used both decoratively and as protection against dust.

Embossed fabric: Fabric with a textured, indented, and raised patterned surface created with heated engraving rollers. Embossed velvet is among the most common of this type of fabric.

End caps: Finishing caps applied to the end of a curtain rod in lieu of decorative finials.

End stop: A plastic or metal fixing at the end of a track or traverse rod to prevent the curtains sliding off.

Espanole bolts: Opening, closing, and locking mechanism for centre-opening French doors or windows.

Euro pleat: A pleat that has two or three folds and is tacked within 1.25cm (½in) from the top.

Eyelet: A small metal ring pressed into fabric, creating an opening through which cords or laces may be inserted.

Face cloth: The front of a curtain; the decorative or main fabric.

Fanlight: A window over a door or another window, especially one in the form of a semi-circle or a half-ellipse.

Fascia: Any relatively broad, flat, horizontal surface, set over a window to cover a curtain heading or blind fixing.

Feed dogs: On a sewing machine, this is a plate with saw-shaped teeth that moves fabric through the machine. As the needle stitches, the feed dogs grab the fabric, moving it under the presser foot.

Festoon blind: see Ruched blind.

Finial: The decorative end pieces of a metal or wooden curtain rod or pole, used to finish the ends and keep the curtains from sliding off.

Finished length: The distance from the top to the bottom of a completed curtain.

Flame-retardant fabrics: Fabrics that are inherently flame resistant, such as wool, or those that are treated with a finish to slow their burn rate.

Flat weave: A process of weaving in which the weft threads are not carried the full width of the fabric but woven in as needed in the design. The weft threads also completely cover the warp and the resulting fabric is reversible. Also known as tapestry or kilim.

Flemish heading: A goblet-pleated heading in which the pleats are linked across the base by a cord.

Floor cloth: Painted canvas that is bound or folded-under around the edges and used on a hard floor instead of a rug.

French pleat: A curtain heading with triple pleats separated by flat expanses of cloth between them. Also known as a pinch pleat.

Frieze: The area of a wall between a picture rail and the ceiling, often painted or moulded with a repeating decorative design.

Fullness: The multiple of extra fabric added to the finished width of window treatments to create a full appearance. The standard fullness for custom window treatments is 2½ to 3 times the total width of the treatment.

Fusible webbing: A see-through material based on glue or plastic that may be sticky on both sides, or only one side. It usually requires ironing to activate the stickiness, but some may also be sewn. It is available in rolls, by the metre, or smaller pieces.

Fustian: Heavy-duty down-proof calico with a close, ribbed or twill weave. It is used as an inner cover for down-filled cushions, bolsters, and so on.

Gaufrage: A method of embossing fabrics. The technique can also be used to emboss leather.

Gimp: A flat trimming of silk, wool, or other cord, sometimes stiffened with wire and often containing metallic threads, used for trimming curtains, decorative tablecloths, and so on.

Glazing bars: Wooden or metal strips within a window frame that separate one pane of glass from another.

Goblet pleats: A curtain heading with rounded, goblet-shaped pleats. The tubes of the pleats may be wrapped and sewn around cylindrical forms and tacked at the bottom to form the goblet; often filled with wadding.

Grain: The direction of the threads in a fabric.

Grommet: A reinforced eyelet, as in cloth or leather, through which a fastener may be passed.

Half-tester: A shallow rectangular bed canopy with curtains at either side to create a three-dimensional effect.

Hand: The qualities of a fabric, especially with respect to how it feels to the touch.

Header: The ruffled edge above a rod-pocket curtain heading.

Heading: The top edge of a curtain, which can be finished with tape, pins, rings, tabs, pleats, or other means and by which the curtain panel is suspended from a track, rod or pole.

Heading tape: Any of a variety of tapes with cords that produce shirred, pleated, smocked, or other styled curtain headings.

Herringbone: A twill weave produced by alternating the direction of a diagonal pattern within a woven cloth. Also a hand stitch used to join interlining or neaten raw edges.

Hobbled Roman blind: A Roman blind with fixed, soft, regularly spaced, horizontal folds.

Holdback: See Boss.

Holland blind: Finely woven canvas used for roller blinds in the 18th and 19th centuries to protect furnishings and carpets from damaging sunlight. It is always a natural colour.

Hook-and-loop tape: A double tape with one strip featuring a looped surface, the other a hooked surface. These catch when the two strips are pressed together. It may be sewn or ironed onto a surface. Also called touch-and-close tape; Velcro is a popular brand.

Hue: A particular gradation of a colour; a shade or tint.

Interfacing: A stiffener fabric sewn or fused onto a fabric to give it body.

Interlining: A soft material, such as bump or domett, sewn between the face fabric of a curtain and its lining to add bulk, improve draping and handling, and acting as insulation.

Inverted pleat: Also known as a kick pleat, an inverted pleat is formed like a box pleat in reverse so the edges of the pleat meet to conceal the underlying fabric. It is often used at the corners of bed skirts or the skirts of sofas or chairs.

Italian stringing: A technique that allows curtain panels that have a fixed heading to be raised or lowered by means of a cord strung through small rings sewn in a curved formation on the back of the curtain.

Jabot: An ornamental cascade or tapered piece of fabric that drapes down on either side of a swag or valance for a decorative effect.

Jacquard: A special loom or the method employed in the weaving of a complex figured fabric known as a jacquard fabric.

Jalousie window: A window comprised of many slats of glass that open and close using a crank.

Jardinière curtains: Sheer curtains, sometimes made of lace, which arch along the middle of the lower edge allowing part of the window to be revealed.

Jute: A fibrous material from the stem of the corchorus plant, which is processed to make strong yarn for weaving burlap or hessian as a backing for carpets and other decorative elements.

Kapok: Loose fibres from a tree, used to create wadding for stuffing pillows and other decorative elements.

Kick pleat: See Inverted pleat.

Kilim: A tapestry-woven, pileless rug or other textile with geometric designs in rich, brilliant colours from various parts of the Middle East, eastern Europe and Turkestan. Also known as kelim.

Lace: A fine openwork fabric made by knotting or twisting threads to form an intricate pattern against a net-like background material. Usually made of cotton in white or cream and used as an edging.

Lambrequin: A shaped, stiff surround for a window, which extends along the top like a pelmet and continues down the sides. It usually has decorative shaping and is covered with fabric.

Leaded lights: Square or diamond-shaped panes of glass set in lead to form a window.

Leading edge: The front vertical edges of a pair of curtains, which meet and cross over in the middle when the panels are closed.

Lining: A secondary fabric sewn into or attached to the back of curtains or used to back fabrics of other soft furnishings. A lining provides extra strength, protects the face fabric from fading, and enhances drapability. It is usually made of finely woven cotton sateen but is also available in other fabrics that provide extra insulation or black-out capability.

Lintel: A beam carrying the load over a door or window.

Linterfelt: A term for the fibrous waste of cotton bump or wadding.

Lip: The tape edge attached to readymade piping or self-welt cord to be used as a seam allowance.

Loose covers: Fabric covers that can be slipped over sofas and chairs to protect their upholstery fabric or give them a different seasonal look. Also called slipcovers.

Louvred blinds: Blinds with wide vertical slats, which can be made of wood, metal plastic or woven fabric.

Master carrier: The central carriers of a traverse rod or track with arms that overlap in the centre.

Mercerized cloth: Woven cotton, linen, or cellulose-fibre cloth that has been treated with a cold, concentrated solution of caustic soda to cause an irreversible swelling of fibres, which imparts surface lustre.

Metre or yardstick: A metal or wooden stick marked with centimeters or inches, or fractions thereof, used for measuring.

Moiré: A variation of the calendering process in which specially engraved rollers are applied to the surface of a fabric to create a watermarked effect, often on taffeta cloth.

Monochromatic scheme: A colour scheme that incorporates elements with different shades or values of a single colour.

Mullion: The vertical bars made of wood or stone that divide the glazing of a window.

Muntin: The vertical and horizontal wood strips that separate panes of glass in a window.

Nap: The fibrous surface or pile of a fabric, which affects a cloth's apparent colour and the way it reflects light.

Opening light: The opening part of a window.

Open-weave: Another name for a loosely woven sheer.

Patio windows: Usually metal-framed, sliding windows that allow easy access to a patio, porch, or terrace.

Pelmet: A shaped, stiffened piece of fabric mounted at the top of a window over curtains to hide a track.

Pencil pleats: A tightly gathered curtain heading with narrow, densely packed pleats. Usually made with a heading tape.

Picture rail: A simple beading or shallow shelf running around the walls of a room below the ceiling beneath the frieze level to support pictures suspended by means of hooks and wires.

Pile: Fabric with a tufted or looped surface on the face of the cloth.

Pinch pleat: See French pleat.

Pin hooks: Shaped metal pins that are pointed on one side and hooked on the other, enabling them to be inserted into the pleats of a curtain heading and hooked onto the carriers of a track or traverse rod. Also called drapery hooks.

Piping: A neat edging for seams of loose covers, cushions, and so on, made by covering cord with seamed strips of cloth cut on the bias, and sandwiching it between the fabrics to be joined.

Plantation shutters: Louvred internal shutters traditionally made from wood. The louvres are opened and closed by a metal rod.

Plush: A fabric with a deep pile, which is similar to velvet but less dense.

Pouffe: Material gathered into a bunch; a very firmly stuffed drum- or cube-shaped cushion or hassock, for use on the floor.

Portière curtain and rod: A curtain that hangs behind a door to completely cover the opening and ward out draughts. It is suspended from a special rod that rises and falls as the door opens.

Printed cloth: Any cloth that has been coloured with a printed design, either by hand or mechanical means.

Provençal print: Any French country print with brightly coloured small motifs, often paisleys and floral designs, usually on cotton or oilcloth.

Railroad: To turn a fabric sideways so the selvage runs horizontally across the treatment rather than vertically up and down.

Raw edge: The cut edge of a fabric, which often frays and can be neatened in various ways.

Receding colour: A cool colour that appears to move away from you, creating the impression of an enlarged space.

Recess: A niche into which a window is set.

Repeat: The full length of a vertical fabric design, measured between the two points where the pattern starts, or is repeated.

Return: The flat outside edge of a curtain covering the area between the front of the rod or track and the wall. The distance between the face of the pole, rod, or track and the wall.

Reveal: The side walls of a window niche.

Roller blind: A simple flat window treatment on a cylindrical roller, often operated by a spring mechanism or beaded cord.

Roller or cylinder printing: A printing process involving engraved metal rollers to print a design on fabric. Originally developed for engravings, then developed for wallpaper and eventually for fabric in the 17th century.

Roman blind: A tailored fabric blind, which produces lateral pleats when raised and is flat when closed.

Rosette: A small decorative rose made of ribbon or fabric used as a finishing motif on curtain headings, tiebacks, cushions and other elements. It can be knife-pleated, choux, or bow style.

Rouleau fastening: A fastening made with a rolled piece of cloth.

Ruched blind: A fabric blind gathered into soft folds by means of shirring tape or rings and cords at the back. Also called a festoon blind.

Sash window: A window with two glazed panels that slide open on runners without extending outwards or inwards; it is also called a double-hung window.

Scalloped heading or edging: This is a heading or edging with deep semi-circular cutouts; in the case of a heading the scallops slip onto the curtain rod or pole.

Seam allowance: Extra fabric left on the narrow edge of a seam to allow for fabric fraying. It needs to be calculated in the fabric quantities required for the project.

Seam ripper: A small tool with a pointed metal cutting tip for unpicking seams and stitches.

Selvage: The firmly woven and bound side edges of a fabric, which run parallel to the warp along the length of the fabric. If the fabric is patterned it may indicate the fabric repeat to aid in matching patterns. If widths are joined to create curtain panels it may need to be notched, trimmed, or weighted to prevent puckering.

Shade: see Blind.

Sheers: Thin, translucent fabrics, such as lace, lawn, voile, muslin, or net, used to filter light and provide privacy at a window, or used as bed canopies or table skirts.

Shirring: A method of gathering fabric by means of tiny stitches, which are pulled to form tight little pleats. Shirring may also be done with specially designed corded tapes.

Shutters: Window coverings made of wood or metal that are set on hinges on the interior or on the exterior of a window.

Sidelights: Narrow windows, usually placed on either side of a door.

Silk screen printing: A printing process similar to stencilling in which the dye is forced through a prepared screen of fine mesh.

Sill: The horizontal ledge of the bottom edge of a window or door.

Skirt: A term for a dressy table cover or frill around the base of a bed or upholstered piece of furniture.

Skirting board: A narrow band of wood or moulding running around the walls at the bottom of edge of a room next to the floor. Also called baseboard.

Slipcover: See Loose cover.

Slot heading: A heading sewn along the top of a curtain panel, allowing the panel to be suspended by the fabric. The heading may be made as a casing, slots, loops, or castellations.

Slub: Slightly thicker threads woven into a fabric at irregular intervals to create a textured appearance.

Smocked heading: A curtain heading made with pencil pleats stitched or gathered together at regular points to create a honeycomb pattern or smocked effect. This may be done with heading tape or by hand.

Soffit: The underside of an architectural feature, such as a beam, arch, ceiling, vault, or cornice.

Squab: A flat removable pillow or chair pad used to soften wooden or metal chair seats or backs.

Swag: A decorative top treatment made of a rounded wedge or wedges of fabric, draped into soft folds and mounted above a window, either alone or over curtain panels. It is often used in a complex arrangement including cascades, jabots, or tails.

Synthetic fibres: A group of manmade fibres, used alone or in blends to create fabrics. Some are by-products of petroleum production, such as acrylic, nylon, and polyester; others are made from cellulose, such as acetate, rayon, and viscose.

T-pins: Large pins with T-shaped heads used to hold cloth to an upholstered piece of furniture when cutting out covers.

Tacking thread: Thread, usually in a contrasting colour, used to form tacking stitches before seaming two or more parts of a soft furnishing together. Also called basting thread.

Tails: Folded panels of fabric framing the sides of a swag top treatment.

Tape-gathered heading: A curtain heading formed by specially constructed tapes with cords sewn to the top of the panels. When the cords are pulled, any of various pleat styles can be formed.

Tapestry: A heavy, woven fabric often depicting traditional designs used for upholstery or cushion covers. Tapestries were originally hand-embroidered or woven wall hangings. It also describes a kind or weaving.

Template: A pattern, usually of card, paper, or plastic, used as a guide to trace a design on fabric.

Ticking: A heavy cotton twill fabric used to make casings or coverings for pillows, mattresses, and bolsters. It is tightly woven to prevent fillers, such as feathers, down, or horse hair to penetrate through, and is usually woven with black, red, or blue stripes on an off-white background.

Tint: A value of a colour created by adding white to a pure hue.

Toile: A loose cover pattern cut from an inexpensive fabric to see the effect and make any fit adjustments before the expensive face cloth is cut.

Tone: A mid-tone value of a colour created by adding grey to a pure hue.

Touch-and-close tape: See hook-and-loop tape.

Track: A curtain track with an integrated cord system for opening and closing the curtains.

Transom window: A window above a door; if an exterior door, the transom window is often fixed, if an interior door, it can often be opened either by hinges at the top or bottom, or by rotating about hinges at the middle of its sides. It provided ventilation before forced air heating and cooling systems were developed.

Traverse rod: A decorative curtain rod with a built-in track with cords and carriers that allow curtain panels to be opened over a wide expanse.

Turkey work: A heavy, woven fabric or embroidery made to look like hand-woven rugs from the Middle East.

Valance: A window top treatment made of a panel of fabric that may be gathered, pleated, or flat, and attached to a rod or board mounted above the window.

Value: The weight or strength of a colour, sometimes referred to as a tone.

Velcro: A popular brand of hook-and-loop tape.

Wadding: Cotton, wool, or synthetic fibres, in batts or sheets, used as filling for cushions, quilts or bedcovers. Also called batting.

Wainscot: The wood, especially oak, that is used for panelling interior walls. The name used for the panelling itself.

Wall anchors: Plastic or metal anchors used to secure screws or bolts in to various types of wall surfaces. Often referred to as rawl plugs.

Warp: The lengthwise threads of a fabric.

Warp-faced: A fabric in which most of the warp threads are on the face surface, hiding the weft threads.

Weights: Chain or lead weights sewn into the hem of a curtain to keep it from billowing or puckering.

Weft: The crosswise threads of a fabric interlaced with the warp threads to produce various weaves.

Welting: Decorative cord.

Width: The measurement across a fabric from selvage to selvage.

Worsted: A closely-twisted yarn or thread; fabric made from this yarn – it has a smooth, close-textured surface and no nap.

resources

Beacon Hill
Chelsea Harbour Design
Centre
Chelsea Harbour, Chelsea
London, SW10 0XE
020 7352 0931

Beacon Hill
225 Foxboro Blvd.
Foxboro, MA 02035
800-333-3777
www.beaconhilldesign.com

British Trimmings
Stockport, UK
0161 480 6122
www.britishtrimmings.com

Calico Corners
800-213-6366
www.calicocorners.com

Conso
8701 Red Oak Blvd., Ste 250
Charlotte, NC 28217
800-628-9362
www.conso.com

Country Curtains
800-456-0321
www.countrycurtains.com

Covington Fabrics
New York, NY
212-689-2200

Denver Fabrics
2777 W Belleview Ave
Littleton, CO 80123
303-730-2777
www.denverfabrics.com

Dritz
www.dritz.com

Duralee
1775 Fifth Ave.
Bay Shore, NY 11706
631-273-8800
www.duralee.com

Fabrics and Home
www.fabricsandhome.com
800-582-2624

Fabric En France
www.fabricenfrance.co.uk/store
01721 752280

Fairfield Processing
P.O. Box 1130
Danbury, CT 06813-1130
800-980-8000
www.poly-fil.com

Graber
877-792-0002
www.graberblinds.com

Hanes Fabrics
800-430-8296
www.hanesfabric.com

Husqvarna Viking
VSM (UK) Ltd
Ravensbank House
Ravensbank Drive, Redditch
Worcestershire B98 9NA
01527 519480
www.husqvarnaviking.com/uk

Husqvarna Viking
VSM Sewing Inc.
31000 Viking Parkway
Westlake, OH 44145
440-808-6550
800-358-0001
www.husqvarnaviking.com/us

JAB
A division of Stroheim and
Romann
New York, NY
212 486 1500
www.jab.de

Kirsch
524 W. Stevenson St.
Freeport, IL 61032
800-528-1407
www.kirsch.com

Kravet Fabrics, Inc.
Bethpage, NY
516-293-2000
www.kravet.com

Mokuba
55 W 39th St
New York, NY 10018
212-869-8900
www.mokubany.com

Robert Allen Fabrics
225 Foxboro Blvd.
Mansfield, MA 02035
800-333-3777
www.robertallendesign.com

SeaCloth
203-854 4863 ext 17
www.seacloth.com

Stroheim & Romann
30-30 47th Avenue
New York, NY 11101
718-706-7000
www.stroheim.com

Thibaut
480 Frelinghuysen Avenue
Newark, New Jersey 07114
800-223-0704
www.thibautdesign.com

Umbra
www.umbra.com

Velcro
www.velcro.com

Waverly
800-523-1200
www.waverly.com

index

acknowledgements

A team of knowledgeable people came to my aid to produce this book and several individuals and companies deserve special thanks for their professional efforts, contributions and insight. I'd especially like to thank Christine D'Ascoli of Covington, Janice Langrall of Stroheim & Romann, Sabeen Kahn of Thibaut, Jolie Cross Cohen of Beacon Hill and Robert Allen Design, and Tim Allen of Hanes Fabrics for their insight on decorative home textiles and linings and their generosity in the development of several of the projects that appear in this book. I am also extremely grateful to Julie Morris and Jan Jessup of Calico Corners for sharing their wisdom on many of the technical issues and finer points of well-made soft furnishings. My thanks go, too, to Pam Maffei-Toolan of Waverly for sharing her expertise on textiles.

The Husqvarna Viking sewing machine company has also kept me abreast of the latest developments in sewing machine technology and accessories over the years and I am grateful for the illustrations it provided for the sewing machine accessories section of the book. My gratitude also goes to the Kirsch company for sharing its expertise on curtain hardware and to the Fairfield Processing Corporation for its knowledge on cushion inserts and padding, as well as for both companies' contributions to the development of several projects in the book. Illustrations on page 178-179 courtesy of Husqvarna Viking. For more information please visit **www.husqvarnaviking.com**.

Chris Wagner spent several days sewing and explaining the construction of several of the projects in this book, Lizzie Sanders spent many more illustrating the steps it took to made them, Keith Scott Morton beautifully photographed these soft furnishings—and I'd like to thank all of them for the ways in which they went above above and beyond the call of duty. Arthur Brown, Jo Weeks and Helen Griffin also deserve special thanks for their gracious professionalism and invaluable attention to detail. I am also grateful to Fiona Lindsay for getting the ball rolling, to my dear friend Mary Gilliatt for her kind support along the way, and to my parents, William and Merriam Gorman, for encouraging me to learn to sew at a very young age. Finally, I'd like to express my gratitude to my husband, Anil Nayar, for his patience and support during the many long days it took to research, write and pull together the pieces of this book.

Picture Credits

t = top; b= bottom; r = right; l = left; c = centre
With special thanks to **redcover.com** and the following photographers for additional images: Alun Callender 87tl; 87b; 89tr; 126; 128l; 128r; Bieke Claessens 90; Brian Harrison 66; 71t; Carlos Dominguez 84; Christopher Drake 101; Guglielmo Galvin 38; Huntley Hedworth 67; Henry Wilson 52; 70b; 88b; 89bl; 92tr; Ken Hayden 88tl; Mark Bolton 70t; Nick Carter 69l; Tommy Lennartsson 86r; Winfried Heinze 16; 87tr; 89tl.

The author and publisher would also like to thank the following professional interior designers for their assistance with photography:

Monika Apponyi: 69tl

Michael Banks: 39tr

Roger Banks-Pye: 12r; 19r; 20bl; 24r; 26; 50; 51; 93br; 109tr; 115bl; 135; 136t

Ginger Barber: 35br

Lars Bolander: 30tr

Nancy Braithwate: 10b; 30l; 13b; 20tl; 20tr; 22; 27; 38tr; 39tl; 56; 57; 91tr; 93tr; 110tl; 118; 119; 132tl; 137tr; 146; 147

Robert Clark & Raymond Le Cuyer: 39br; 132bl

Michael de Santis: 154; 155

Christopher Drake: 134 tl; 152; 153

Mary Drysdale: 9; 11t; 11b; 16bl; 17tl; 24l; 26; 28tl; 28br; 33tr; 37br; 38br; 73tr; 86l; 93tl; 103; 104; 111c; 111b; 113; 114br; 115tl; 120; 136bl; 136br; 139tr

Marilyn Glass: 36r; 111tl

Carol Glasser: 18bl; 29t; 91tl; 99; 106; 111tc; 115br; 130tl; 131; 137tl; 140; 141

Mariette Himes Gomez: 13l; 92tl

Richard Holley: 36cll; 114tl

Marie Gouny: 10t; 17tr; 17br; 18c; 28bl; 38cr

Stephen & Gail Huberman: 32tl; 34tl

Beverly Jacomini: 15; 109tl; 130tr; 133tr

Richard Keith Langham: 32r; 139cr

Tonin MacCallum: 23l; 139c

Charlotte Moss: 67tr

Julian Muggeridge: 30br

Brett Nestler: 16tl

Mimi O'Connell: 34bl

Melanie Paine: 6b

Graham Rust: 68

Anna Thomas: 12l; 14tl; 23r; 29b; 31t; 31b; 36bl; 37tr; 66bl; 72tl; 88c; 89br; 115 tr; 115cr; 134tr

Stephanie Vatelot: 14r; 17bl; 19l; 37tl; 46; 47; 48; 132br; 138tl

Sasha Waddell: 8; 18r; 21b; 66tl; 85; 88tr; 92b; 93b; 114bl; 129br; 142; 143; 156

Todhunter Earle Interiors: 35tr

Karen White: 14br; 33br; 36tl; 139tl

Virginia Mae Witbeck: 7

Vincente Wolf: 6l; 13r; 108l; 108r; 134bl; 139b